# SEEING THINGS, FROM SHAKESPEARE TO PIXAR

A technological revolution has changed the way we see things. The story-telling media employed by Pixar Animation Studios, Samuel Beckett, and William Shakespeare differ greatly, yet these creators share a collective fascination with the nebulous boundary between material objects and our imaginative selves. How do the acts of seeing and believing remain linked? Alan Ackerman charts the dynamic history of interactions between showing and knowing in *Seeing Things*, a richly interdisciplinary study which illuminates changing modes of perception and modern representational media.

*Seeing Things* demonstrates that the airy nothings of *A Midsummer Night's Dream*, the Ghost in *Hamlet*, and soulless bodies in Beckett's media experiments, alongside *Toy Story*'s digitally animated toys, all serve to illustrate the modern problem of visualizing, as Hamlet put it, 'that within which passes show.' Ackerman carefully analyses such ghostly appearances and disappearances across cultural forms and contexts from the early modern period to the present, investigating the tension between our distrust of shadows and our abiding desire to believe in invisible realities. *Seeing Things* provides a fresh and surprising cultural history through theatrical, verbal, pictorial, and cinematic representations.

ALAN ACKERMAN is an associate professor in the Department of English at the University of Toronto.

ALAN ACKERMAN

# Seeing Things

## From Shakespeare to Pixar

UNIVERSITY OF TORONTO PRESS
Toronto Buffalo London

ISBN 978-1-4426-4364-2 (cloth)
ISBN 978-1-4426-1210-5 (paper)

Printed on acid-free, 100% post-consumer recycled paper with
vegetable-based inks.

**Library and Archives Canada Cataloguing in Publication**

Ackerman, Alan L. (Alan Louis)
Seeing things : from Shakespeare to Pixar / Alan Ackerman.

Includes bibliographical references and index.
ISBN 978-1-4426-4364-2 (bound). – ISBN 978-1-4426-1210-5 (pbk.)

1. Technology and the arts.   2. Visual communication.   3. Visual
perception.   I. Title.

NX180.T4A35 2011      700.1'05      C2011-903071-3

University of Toronto Press acknowledges the financial assistance to its
publishing program of the Canada Council for the Arts and the Ontario
Arts Council.

 Canada Council   Conseil des Arts        ONTARIO ARTS COUNCIL
for the Arts   du Canada                 CONSEIL DES ARTS DE L'ONTARIO

University of Toronto Press acknowledges the financial support of the
Government of Canada through the Canada Book Fund for its publishing
activities.

For Max and Alice

# Contents

# Acknowledgments

Sections of this book have been published in earlier forms by the University of Toronto Press (2008), *University of Toronto Quarterly* (2005), *Contemporary Literature* (2003), and *Theatre Journal* (2001). I thank these publishers for their permission to reprint revised versions of these essays here.

I gratefully acknowledge the support of the University of Toronto, Department of English, and the Social Sciences and Humanities Research Council of Canada. Sarah Kriger has been an invaluable research assistant. Her broad knowledge of visual technologies and sharp insights into the history and philosophy of science contributed valuably to this book. Thanks also to the diligent efforts and keen enthusiasm of Anna Gallagher-Ross.

At the University of Toronto Press, Richard Ratzlaff nurtured this project from beginning to end. I am very grateful for his warm commitment and clear-eyed editorial guidance. I am indebted as well to the careful efforts of John St James, Laura Jones Dooley, Barbara Porter, and Cynthia Crippen.

For carefully reading and commenting on drafts of various chapters, I warmly thank Sarah Wilson, Jonathan Warren, Martin Puchner, Richard Begam, Louis Kaplan, Alexander Leggatt, and Scott Stevens. Thanks also to Charlie Keil for his advice and insights into the nature of film (and cinema studies). I am indebted beyond measure to Andrea Most, who read every word of this book countless times, always offering constructive criticism, intellectual guidance, and emotional support. This book is a testament to her generous spirit.

Most of all, I thank my children, Max and Alice, who introduced me to the *Toy Story* movies and with whom watching these movies over and over again became a source of infinite pleasure. We have shared the joys of Shakespeare too, reciting the speeches, dressing the parts, and absorbing the plays. Together we sat in the grass for numerous outdoor performances of *A Midsummer Night's Dream*, even as the floodlights misted with rain. Max was born on the dark and stormy night I prepared to give my first lecture on *Hamlet*, profoundly deepening my relationship to this greatest of all plays and connecting it ineluctably for me with the cycles of life (the lecture had to wait for later). Max and Alice have given me new worlds to see and eyes with which to see them.

A version of chapter 1 originally appeared as 'A Spirit of Giving in *A Midsummer Night's Dream*' in *Shakespeare's Comedies of Love: Essays in Honour of Alexander Leggatt*, edited by Karen Bamford and Ric Knowles, 110–25. Toronto: University of Toronto Press, 2008.

A version of chapter 2 originally appeared as 'Visualizing Hamlet's Ghost: The Spirit of Modern Subjectivity.' *Theatre Journal* 53, no. 1 (March 2001): 119–44. © 2001, The Johns Hopkins University Press.

A version of chapter 3 originally appeared as 'Samuel Beckett's *spectres du noir*: The Being of Painting and the Flatness of *Film*.' *Contemporary Literature* 44, no. 3 (Fall 2003): 399–441. © 2003 by the Board of Regents of the University of Wisconsin System. It is reproduced here with revisions courtesy of the University of Wisconsin Press.

A version of chapter 4 originally appeared as 'The Spirit of Toys: Resurrection and Redemption in *Toy Story* and *Toy Story 2*.' *University of Toronto Quarterly* 74, no. 4 (Fall 2005): 895–912.

SEEING THINGS, FROM SHAKESPEARE TO PIXAR

# Introduction: Seeing Things

Betwixt mine eye and heart a league is took,
And each doth good turns now unto the other.

William Shakespeare, Sonnet 47

My approach to seeing things is naive. I want to believe: that Michelangelo's rebellious slave will burst his marble bands; that an open window's radiant light inspires Caravaggio's St Matthew; that Pixar's pixellated toys break and repair. I like to think that when a person leaves the screen or stage he goes into another room or into a landscape glimpsed through a closing door, or when the camera cuts to a listener in a conversation that she is actually reacting to what her partner said. At the same time, I am sceptical, distrustful of shadows and hints of the unseen, troubled by the promise of wonders beyond sensory experience, evidence, and reason's grasp. I know (or say I know) that the screen and canvas are two-dimensional, that depth, like the soul, is a figment of the imagination. There is no *there* in digital animation.

Recently I went to see the new version of Charles Dickens's *A Christmas Carol*, produced in 'Disney Digital 3D' by Robert Zemeckis. Evoking the popular visual technology of Dickens's own day, Zemeckis explains that his rendering of the story is 'phantasmagorical.'[1] Phantasmagoria was the term for popular magic-lantern performances in the 1790s and early 1800s. They used back projections to disguise the use of lanterns, amazing and often terrifying spectators with mysterious, luminous shapes that flew and flickered above their heads.[2] Viewers entered, rather than remained detached from, the field of vision. Cultivating this spirit, Dickens's spectral tale of renewal is about the subjectivity of seeing. It

involves Scrooge as a spectator in visions of his life: images, as Dickens
puts it in the book, 'of which dissolving parts, no outline would be visible in the dense gloom wherein they melted away.'[3] Yet the ghostly
element, in Zemeckis's view, has until now 'never been properly put
on the screen' or 'realized as Dickens intended it.'[4] Although they
made use of lighting and sound effects, make-up, superimpositions, and
even cel-based animation to represent aspects of ghostliness, previous
filmic translations captured neither the unsettling visual experience of
phantasmagoria shows nor, arguably, the spirit of the book, because
directors treated film more as a form of narration than as a medium of
theatricalization, that is, a space of seeing.

Zemeckis's comment raises concerns that are central to my book:
How do we analyse relationships between words and images, translate
stories across media, and assess the power of historical factors in shaping our capacity to imagine? Dolby Laboratories, Inc., which specializes
in three-dimensional movies in digital media, provided Disney with
the technology for A Christmas Carol ('Disney Digital 3D' is only a marketing term). The movie screen on which I had the pleasure of viewing it must have been twenty metres high. Twin projectors launched
Dolby 3D onto the standard, non-silver screen. Digital surround sound
enveloped us. On the Disney website Zemeckis and actor Jim Carrey
comment that the key to viewing the world's 'greatest ghost story' is
that the new format gives the audience the experience of being on a
roller coaster, of moving at 'one hundred million miles an hour.' The
paradigmatic modern ghost story is about speed, and, as the Disney
website makes plain, in content and form it is motivated, like Dickens's
central character, by economic considerations.

In the movie, when the green ghost of Marley erupted with its cash-
boxes and heavy purses wrought in steel through Scrooge's massive
oaken door, it was a really scary experience. But it also indicated a vital
tension between seeing and reading that I wish to explore. It became
frustrating to race (though firmly planted in our stadium-style seats)
again and again past objects on which the eye wished to linger. To be
fair, in its very kineticism this movie aimed to be faithful to the book.
On the one hand, in accordance with a Disney convention, an image
of a leather-bound volume, with title and author's name 'inscribed' on
the cover, opened and closed the picture, implying that the viewer,
like a Victorian reader, occupied a static position in a comfy chair by
the fire. On the other, Dickens too describes the Ghost of Christmas
Present as a disorienting figure of motion: 'The spirit did not tarry

here, but bade Scrooge hold his robe and passing on above the moor, sped whither? ... Again the Ghost sped on,' and so on.[5] In the hour he spends with the second ghost – the most visually demanding of the spirits in a proto-modernist kind of way – zooming through a market-place bursting with the fruits of empire and from city to country and back again, Scrooge struggles to get his bearings: 'It was a long night, if it were only a night; but Scrooge had his doubts of this, because the Christmas Holidays appeared to be condensed into the space of time they passed together.' Even Dickens seems confused; the spirit repre-sents one Christmas (that of 1843), but of course there are innumerable Christmas Holidays within that one. The spirit of the present reveals 'many worlds' from which Scrooge may 'profit.'[6] The phrase 'space of time' suggests a playful way of imagining the ghostliness of both space and time to which the hyper-kinetic 3D visual media later prove pecu-liarly suited. A radical consumer, whose illuminating torch is shaped like Plenty's horn, the spirit of the present is also an object of consump-tion. Its first demand is that Scrooge 'Look upon me!' And 'Scrooge rev-erently did so.'[7] But the many things heaped on the floor of Scrooge's room – turkeys, geese, game, poultry, great joints of meat, sucking-pigs, long wreaths of sausages, mince pies, plum pudding, etc. – then van-ish instantly, and by the hour's end, 'Scrooge looked about him for the Ghost, and saw it not.'[8] The spirit of the present is the spirit of moder-nity, by which I mean a world view that arose in post-medieval Europe. It is not continuous with the past but always, uncontrollably, in transi-tion towards some unrealized future. It is marked by an awareness of its own position in history. It is mobile (socially, geographically, and so on), and it is characterized by abstraction, the sense that the world is not inherently whole but composed of discrete or separable parts (whether turkeys, geese, and game or pounds and pence) that cohere in the eye of the observer or appear organized by something unseen, like the invisible hand of Adam Smith. Dickens's spirit, prefigured by two-and-a-half centuries in Doctor Faustus's sweet Mephistopheles, repre-sents the unrepressed desires of an all-consuming culture with an eye on both profit and delight.

This assumption is basic to Zemeckis's belief that Dickens's world is our world, not only in its capitalistic aims but also in the arguably seamless translation of its themes to new media. Zemeckis suggests that what Dickens made in words, for the mind's eye, was all along *meant* for 3D animation, a spirit of Christmases yet to come. Of course, from the vantage point of a culture saturated with motion pictures, it is impossible to say whether he would have recognized his ghost story in Disney's 3D spectacle. Most people would agree that meaning is a product of one's technological and economic milieus. Dickens, from his travels on steam locomotives and wave-tossed ships, was able to imagine an experience of speed and vertigo. In form and content, his story reflects a contemporary tension between the desire for a stable spectator-position and the rejuvenating thrill of being caught up in the action. It is organized by the visible – invisible logic of capitalism, the temporal structure of credit (from *credere,* to believe) and debt, and the relationship it entails between borrowers and lenders, the portability of money and the invisibility of value or, what Jacques Derrida calls 'the furtive and ungraspable visibility of the invisible, or an invisibility of a visible X, that *non-sensuous sensuous* of which [Marx's] *Capital* speaks.'[9]

Hopefully kinder and more generous, we are all, nonetheless, like Scrooge, products of a visually hyperactive and confusing age, caught by the spectral, if not invisible, hand of commerce. (Disney's profits dwarf those of Scrooge and Marley.) Visual reproductions and diverse media, each more vivid and spectacular than the last, compete for our attention on every city street. Driving on expressways around the major cities of North America becomes ever more intensely distracting because, in addition to videos *in* the car, billboards above the highway now include massive three-dimensional installations and JumboTrons delivering live-action movie clips. Few would dispute Guy Debord, the late French Marxist filmmaker and cultural critic, who argued that in contemporary society, 'all of life ... presents itself as an immense accumulation of *spectacles.'*[10] Furthermore, as everyone knows these days, no matter where you live, you are subjected to visual technologies that remain themselves invisible. Surveillance cameras, X-ray machines in hospitals and airports, magnetic resonance imaging, satellite imaging systems such as Google Maps: all of these record and represent the most intimate details of our lives – in some cases, our very bodily interiors – though we never see the images they produce. We all become, as Ophelia says of Hamlet, both observers and observed. Locating objects of vision in the human interior also has an impact on the world we think we see.

Art and film theorist Rudolf Arnheim writes that 'visual perception lays the groundwork of concept formation.'[11] In the 1960s he described what we all know today, that in making sense of the world, the mind and eye do not divide but share their labour: 'The mind, reaching beyond the stimuli received by the eyes directly and momentarily, operates with the vast range of imagery available through memory and organizes a total lifetime's experience into a system of visual concepts.' This operation can be traced to the foundational narratives of the Western tradition. Erich Auerbach's important book *Mimesis*, for instance, begins with a famous scene from Homer's *Odyssey*. Home at last, the disguised Odysseus wins the goodwill of his wife, Penelope. She then instructs his old housekeeper Eurycleia to bathe his feet. The noble wanderer sits by the hearth and turns towards the shadows. Homer says that as the nurse 'started to bathe her master ... she knew in a flash the scar – that old wound made years ago by a boar's white tusk.'[12] How did she know it? Before answering that question, the poet digresses to tell the story of the scar because images and objects need stories to be known. Then, 'as the old nurse cradled his leg and her hands passed down, she felt it, knew it, suddenly let his foot fall – down it dropped in the basin – the bronze clanged, tipping over, spilling water across the floor.'[13] She raises her hand to touch his face. Couched in narrative, the vision is palpable.

Auerbach emphasizes the remarkable clarity with which the action is externalized in the poem: the servant's cry of joy, the way she drops the traveller's foot into the basin and the water spills over, the whispered threats and endearments, and so on. Homer tells the reader that Odysseus takes the old woman by the throat with his right hand to keep her from speaking and, at the same time, draws her closer to him with his left. 'Clearly outlined, brightly and uniformly illuminated,' writes Auerbach, 'men and things stand out in a realm where everything is visible.' But how can *everything* be visible, even in the mind's eye? Language can present visual images in a way that painting and even film cannot. That visualizing capacity is part of what Plato recognized as the poet's mimetic power. Yet, as literary theorist Peter Brooks notes, 'Fictions have to lie in order to tell the truth: they must foreshorten, summarize, perspectivize, give an illusion of completeness from fragments.'[14] So, to follow Auerbach's description of the *Odyssey*, filling 'both the stage and the reader's mind completely,' in a 'fully externalized form, visible and palpable in all their parts,' the Homeric style 'knows only a foreground, only a fully illuminated objective present.' Of course, the genius of the Homeric style and its influence on later mimetic techniques are inextricable from the tradition that the poet, Homer, is blind.[15] The stage is a metaphor. Auerbach's description of vision is figurative. Everything may be illuminated, but the scene occurs in shadows. Recognition happens by touch (as if the nurse too were blind). The perceptual act is only the most recent phase of a history of acts, performed in the past and surviving in memory. It epitomizes what Arnheim calls 'the paradox of seeing a thing as complete, but incompletely.'[16]

Thinking and seeing have been linked since the earliest days of Greek philosophy, but it is vital to note that Jewish, Muslim, and, later, Protestant prohibitions against visual representation (not only depictions of God but also figural realism more broadly) are essential both to the development of an abstract, monotheistic theology and a crucial, anti-illusionist strand of modernity's form of critical reason. Auerbach acknowledges as much in the opening chapter of *Mimesis* by contrasting the total visibility of Homer with the obscurantism of the Hebrew Bible's Elohist. The distinction and interplay between thought and sensibility, imagination and intuition, which are central to Kant's 'critiques,' deeply inform modern notions of perception. To see or not to see: that is the question around which I have organized the following pages. The idiom of ghosts and spirits pervades this wide-ranging study, illuminating the modern problem of representing human interiority and enabling a comparison of modes of representation within richly detailed and diverse contexts. For instance, the problem of seeing everything and nothing at the same time is expressed nowhere more beautifully than in the closet scene in *Hamlet* after the indoor appearance of the Ghost. Hamlet asks his bewildered mother, 'Do you see nothing there?' And she replies: 'Nothing at all, yet all that is I see' (3.4.136–7).[17] This spectacular line is formally perfect, a verbal mirror image whose subject is seeing. The chiasmic reflection of 'you see' / 'I see,' interrogative and declarative, centres on 'Nothing at all,' as if *nothing* had the transparency of glass. Of course, it doesn't. Shakespeare's play and its critical history famously represent the theological confusion (Is it a Catholic play or a Protestant play? Is the Ghost from purgatory or a spirit of the damned?) that turns on early modernity's battle over visual culture, the Renaissance's invention of perspective, and the Reformation's destruction of iconography. At the centre of every (spectral) vision is a nothing that is something.

*Seeing Things, from Shakespeare to Pixar* is inspired by my ordinary way of negotiating this visual paradox. By ordinary I mean that I think of seeing things in a way that is not only both naive and sceptical, but also functional, not metaphysical. I do not attempt to define vision in a unified or essentialist way, but through the lenses of multiple, historical world views. The essays in this book respond, partly and indirectly, to my dissatisfaction with the grim disillusionments of critical theories of the Enlightenment. It is not that I disagree with Horkheimer and Adorno or with Foucault and their many acolytes that the ideal of reason tended to subvert its own promise or that the detached gaze is an instrument of (hidden) power. I am sympathetic, from my own historical vantage point, to the Frankfurt School's critique of the illusion and abstraction that characterized the supposedly clarifying philosophical and empirical movements of the eighteenth century. But there is something oppressive about cultural criticism that asserts uncanny insight into the organization of our most personal assumptions and that denies spontaneity to our perceptions and freedom to our moral lives – the feeling, to paraphrase Freud, that we are robbed of our own eyes.[18] Do we still need to be told that the Enlightenment had its occlusions; that it was superseded by a culture of surveillance; or that vision is predicated on the interplay of clarity and obscurity, presence and absence? When a prominent theatre scholar suggests that the 'action of realist plays often conforms to [a] tyrannical closure of the stage,' I don't know what she is talking about. 'Like a totalitarian political system,' she says, 'the realistic stage operates on the principle of total visibility ... It suggests that everything that is meaningful can be shown, can happen right before our eyes.'[19] Surely this take on realism, a metonymic mode of representation, is mistaken and misleading.

Every spectator knows not only that the stage picture is partial but also that realism is based on a way of seeing things that empowers the individual subject. Ibsen's *Doll House,* that ur-text of domestic realism, begins with the word 'Hide' ('Gem juletræet godt' or 'Hide the Christmas tree well').[20] Later in the play Doctor Rank, with a nod to the 'invisibility cloaks' (or 'invisibility hats': 'usynligheds-hatten')[21] of his cinematic descendents, says that when he returns for future masquerades he will be invisible, by which he means more than dead. He too will become something that is nothing. His absence, signified by a visiting card with a black cross over his name ('Der står et sort kors over navnet'), is a condition of the famous final scene in which Nora recognizes that she has been a doll and wishes to escape her husband's (and her own former) idealizing vision of the world; as with Rank, that means absenting herself from the visual reality of the stage. Even the great empiricist John Locke acknowledged that absences of some things cause effects in the mind. In *An Essay Concerning Human Understanding* he appeals to 'everyone's own Experience, whether the Shadow of a Man, though it consists in nothing but the Absence of Light (and the more the Absence of Light is, the more discernible is the Shadow) does not, when a Man looks on it, cause as clear and positive an idea in the Mind, as Man himself, though covered over with clear Sunshine?'[22] The 'colour' black is caused by an absence of light or, in painting, by a combination of pigments that absorb but do not give off light. Balancing the positive causes of phenomena with the real power of absence, Locke aims for a balance between a philosophical and a common-sense understanding of seeing things. In *Realist Vision,* Peter Brooks, who traces his own enterprise in part to Locke, finds that realism, from the nineteenth-century novel to reality TV, arises from 'our desire to play, and in playing to assert that we master the world, and therefore have a certain freedom in it.'[23] To achieve some measure of freedom, like Ibsen's Nora, Pixar's Buzz Lightyear, or Jake Sully, the part-alien, part-human hero of James Cameron's 3D melodrama *Avatar,* we must first see ourselves as toys, model figures, or things that we can play with, manipulate, and examine, creating discrete sites of creativity in worlds otherwise beyond our control.

Realism is a mode of visual and literary representation that privileges sight among the other senses because it is supposedly the most reliable or objective guide to the world that affects us. Ordinary vision is inseparable from a world of ordinary things, and, in studying 'realist vision,' Brooks says, 'thing-ism' is really his subject (a coinage he derives from an etymology of realism: *res-ism*). Realism is a way of comprehending the hard materiality of a non-idealist world. The impulse of realism, to handle the things of the world as if they were toys, is still much with us, but it is also countered, as it was in the nineteenth century, by fantasies of visual sensation that lack concreteness altogether: notions of a noumenal ego, of human potential, and utopian investments in the 'magic' of theatrical performance, which involve imaginative ways of seeing things, if not outright projections.[24] Much new critical literature has expended itself on things. I hesitate to use the word *theory* here because its visual etymology implies speculation, but critical literature on the topic has also been theoretical in this sense. In his compelling study *The Stage Life of Props,* Andrew Sofer shows that physical objects onstage are not static insofar as their meaning changes in dynamic and meaningful relationship with the audience and the performers. Spectators can study props as they do the inner lives of fictional characters, yet props maintain a material reality – and are always embedded in a larger material culture – even in the absence of symbolic or metaphysical contexts.[25] Props both impersonate other things and perform as objects in themselves.

Drawing on Heidegger's distinction between objects and things, Bill Brown claims that things pressure us to find the subject within the object. In his article 'Thing Theory,' he charts a new model of cultural materialism, but, though he insists on the materiality of things, Brown focuses on the 'meaning' or what he elsewhere calls 'the idea of things.'[26] The things that interest Brown generally have no manifestation outside the world of fiction. In 'How to Do Things with Things (A Toy Story),' he suggests a paradigm shift in thinking about animated objects based on the difference between traditional, hand-drawn technology and computer animation. He notes that Disney's *Toy Story* was the first full-length film to be generated wholly by computer. But he does not investigate how media technologies themselves fit into the picture. Reading only the movie's content (the dramatized tension between novelty and obsolescence), he finds it nostalgic and anachronistic. Elsewhere, he shows how *using* toys, such as a Charlie McCarthy puppet in Shawn Wong's novel *Homebase*, creates meaning. But in what sense is the digital movie also a thing for use? Brown compares fictional things across media or 'texts' without differentiating the technology and media in which they are animated.[27] Theatres, novels, film, and digital movies enable richly different experiences of things. This book shows that it matters that things onstage are both part of the fictional world and actual things, unlike the things in novels, though books too are things in a special sense.

According to Brown's 'material epistemology,' every object embodies a human history, and he says that the importance of *things* has developed with the technologies of mass production. It is no doubt true that mass production, the subject of my last chapter, changed the manufacturing landscape, but is it fair to characterize pre-industrial society as *not* obsessed with things? I address this question in a chapter on *A Midsummer Night's Dream*. The play opens with a speech precisely about the smallest things, which a vexed father believes have 'stolen the impression' of his daughter's 'fantasy.' I want to honour the power and the pervasiveness of 'shaping fantasies,' something Duke Theseus fails to do in *A Midsummer Night's Dream*, while at the same time acknowledging what Theseus calls the 'local habitation' in which 'aery nothing' becomes something.[28] Recent digital technology raises some similar questions to those I find in Shakespeare. Unlike the characters in traditional animation, the characters of *Toy Story*, the subject of my last chapter, began as actual things (real-life maquettes) that were then scanned into a computer. So, in a sense, those digital toys are more *thingy* than hand-drawn cartoon characters. Furthermore, animating things in a computer program employs a dimension and the ability to manipulate things (even if virtual) that drawing the illusion of depth in two dimensions, as in cel-based or hand-drawn animation, does not. Space and 3D animated characters exist in the sense that animators see the virtual dolls and 'sets' stored inside a computer, similar to the virtual page on which my Word document is written, as if it were a real 'page' inside the computer that I can call up and close instead of a string of 1s and 0s, circuits switched on and off. CG/computer animation entails animating a rigged 3D model (a digital three-dimensional sculpture containing an anatomically correct skeleton), while 2D (hand-drawn, or 'cut-out' shapes) involves drawing the shapes as needed and then photographing at least two pictures of each drawing.[29]

It has become conventional wisdom that we are in the midst of a technological revolution that has changed the way we see things and understand seeing. This revolution seems to have begun roughly with the turn of the nineteenth century, and there is no end in sight. My chapter on nineteenth-century interpretations of Hamlet's Ghost also advances this view. But, assuming that 'things' trace paths in time and space, today we must ask how animated time and space differ from real time and space. Although the time and space suggested by any kind of filmic medium is an illusion in a way that stage space is not, it retains key affinities. As James Stewart, the creator of the 3D advertisements for *Avatar*, has said, the 'science of film language,' which includes the 'language of depth,' must also take into account spectators' physical limitations. 'I can put things as far off the screen as I want,' he explains, 'but I have to consider the eye muscles. In 3-D, your eyes are working more, your brain is working more.'[30] Moving beyond the old polarized glasses that enable the eye to create 3D images, a newly developed lenticular lens, which will soon make the glasses obsolete, includes row upon row of tiny lenses that deflect one image to the left eye and one to the right. That technological development does not, however, obviate the old language of depth; on the contrary, it employs and expands it.

I do not propose an alternative to the proliferating 'discourses of vision'[31] that have characterized academic studies of visual culture, but this book does consider what it means to take visual objects *on their own terms*. What are their terms? As Barbara Johnson observes in her marvellous book *Persons and Things*, there are (at least) three dimensions that define relations between persons and things: the reality of desire, the reality of materiality, and the reality of rhetoric. 'Each of these domains,' she writes, 'has an image of the relation between persons and things that ignores the others.'[32] Respecting this schematic arrangement, and particularly its points of conspicuous ignoring, I nonetheless turn my attention to the spaces in which dimensions touch or overlap. Without rejecting phenomenology, as Foucault does, *Seeing Things* situates observing subjects in relation to particular discursive practices, rather than focusing on the *Ding an sich*, Kant's term for 'thing in itself,' which, he believed, the mind can never access directly but can only cognize as appearances made possible by our structures of thought, or 'what we ourselves put into them.'[33] *Ding an sich* became such a loaded term that most philosophy and art of the past two hundred years can be read as a dialogue extending or rejecting Kant's characterization of the relationship between consciousness and phenomena. *Seeing Things* is a literary, cultural, and historical study of the way artists and critics represent details of experience at the intersections of the abstract and the concrete. In diverse contexts and forms, words and images and ideas of spirit and ghosts have epitomized that experience. From Hamlet's father to Jacob Marley, they demand to be understood, and suggest that ultimate understanding is impossible in this material world.

Embodied on the stage or impressed in celluloid or in print, spirits leave traces for our senses to perceive and demand to be remembered or reassembled in our brains and actions. Louis Kaplan's book *The Strange Case of William Mumler, Spirit Photographer* tells the literally fantastic story of a nineteenth-century fad known as spirit photography, a form of visual entertainment that has recently been rediscovered, commodified, and raised to the level of 'high art.'[34] In the early 1860s William Mumler developed a process for producing spiritual photographs that involved photo-electrotype plates and combination or double printing from several negatives. Capitalizing on the mid-nineteenth-century doctrine of Spiritualism, Mumler's work became immensely popular before being subjected to a lawsuit that aimed but failed to determine the exact role of Mumler's hand (i.e., fraud). In his dark room he produced images, not only of persons who clearly had an indexical relation to the film, but also of spiritual loved ones that hovered about them in the pictures. Spirit photographs in the 1860s and 1870s, such as one of Mary Todd Lincoln with the spirits of her departed husband, Abraham, and son Tad laying hands upon her shoulders, offered visual access to 'sensible communion,' but they also raised basic questions about entertainment, money making, and technical manipulations in the artist's or technician's studio.[35]

Whether generated by the Mumler process or by computers, which don't leave traces on film but also require the human mind to extrapolate from bits of information, technological developments in visual culture contribute to new ways of thinking about the human subject as they are framed in legal cases, reviews, and new stories. New ways of seeing things both shape and are shaped by particular discursive frameworks. Literary scholars use the Greek term *ekphrasis* for verbal representations of visual art (such as Homer's description of Achilles' shield) in order to suggest forms of translation between media. This term taps into long-standing disputes about artistic hierarchies. Kant, for instance, ranked poetry highest among the arts because 'it lets the mind feel its ability – free, spontaneous, and independent of natural determination – to contemplate and judge phenomenal nature as having . . . aspects that nature does not on its own offer in experience either to sense or to the understanding.'[36] Visual experience is a passive sensation, he believed, but understanding is discursive. So, in a vital sense, language enables us to see things. In Kant's view, poetry plays critically or self-reflexively with illusion and, therefore, does not use illusion to deceive us.

Recent theorists have questioned this ekphrastic logic, the supposed autonomy of the individual mind, and the privilege accorded to words over images. Art historian W.J.T. Mitchell comments that 'no amount of words can ever duplicate the experience of seeing an image.'[37] Mitchell may be right, but the overdetermined word 'duplicate' suggests the implicit political agenda in what he regards as tensions between verbal and visual representations (his book, *Picture Theory*, was inspired by the trend of seeing power in images, epitomized by a 1988 NEH report). Today digital animation, which is produced by a computer language, indicates that the conceptual diversity of verbal, visual, and other languages can be overdrawn. For instance, the 'language' of mathematics (i.e., the ability to translate motion, mass, volume, and space into algebraic notation) is vital to the causal power in 3D animation.[38] Ultimately, if we push the difference between words and images far enough it can seem to be grounded in nothing. Readers and viewers who follow a thread of aesthetics that aims to resolve the tension between empiricism and rationalism, and winds its way through Walter Pater, Benedetto Croce, Clement Greenberg, and even Michael Fried, may be hostile to the notion that images and words always require translation by means of other images and words. Though gifted with words themselves, each of these writers sought to divorce visual art from other humanist concerns or, in Fried's case, from 'theatricality,' and to see things as they really are. Although these authors have influenced this book, my approach is ekphrastic (the book, for instance, contains no visual images, only words). Like my teacher Elaine Scarry, I marvel at the process by which an action becomes a substance or 'fleeting gestures become materials with shape, weight, and color.'[39] Knowing that there are no facts independent of interpretation, I train my eyes on interpreters of theatrical, verbal, cinematic, and pictorial objects across the centuries. This approach to things is also rhetorical. It investigates structures of perspectives, processes of persuasion and identification, and treats language and vision dramatically, as modes of symbolic action. It considers how, in Hippolyta's rejoinder to Theseus in *A Midsummer Night's Dream*, spectators' minds are 'transfigur'd so together' that they 'More witnesseth than fancy's images.'[40]

It has become common to lump positivism and scientific scepticism with a dogmatic rationalism, but, following William James, whose studies in painting, psychology, and philosophy shaped his pragmatist understanding of truth, I regard the theory/practice opposition and related epistemological anxieties, detailed by theatre studies professor Shannon Jackson, to be both overdrawn and counterproductive.[41] They result largely from a residual Cartesianism that insists on making a problem of the relation of the mind and the world. Of course, it is hard to find a philosopher, psychoanalyst, novelist, or playwright of the twentieth century who does not attack the Cartesian model that equates seeing with being.[42] Like Rudolf Arnheim's theory of visual thinking, Merleau-Ponty's neo-Hegelian synthesis of the relationship between the visible and the invisible, eye and mind, emerges vitally from his dispute with the Cartesian dualism of body and soul. In particular, he isolates Descartes's critique of illusion and his rational reconstruction of the visual domain. 'How crystal clear everything would be in our philosophy,' Merleau-Ponty writes, 'if only we could exorcise these specters, make illusions or object-less perceptions out of them, keep them on the edge of a world that does not equivocate!'[43] What interests me is not a philosophical way of resolving the visible – invisible struggle, but the representation of struggle itself between subjects and objects of vision, and its practical consequences. As a spectator to these theoretical debates, I imagine through a variety of cultural lenses how other people see things; the process not simply by which they see but by which we may be able or unable to share those visions. This approach comes from my earliest experiences of seeing myself seeing. When

I was a child riding in my parents' station wagon through the streets of Pittsburgh, I gazed out the window and worried that my vision might be unique. If my parents turned their heads from the front seat, would they see the same soot-streaked red brick house, the same black lamp post and jutting mast arms that I saw? Of course, if they asked me what I was looking at, I would have said, nothing. Did they have the same experience of vision that I had? When they looked through the window, how did they understand what they saw?

Rather than a Cartesian or solipsistic investigation into my own experience seeing things, therefore, this collection of essays arises from a perception of, and interest in, the multiplicity of perspectives by which our world takes shape. One result of this approach is that the essays cohere around common themes but not a single argument; they are about the experience of historical and, more fundamentally, personal difference. Seeing things is a social phenomenon. My children, with whom I have watched particular movies, from *Toy Story* to *A Christmas Carol*, many, many times, and my perception of their eyes opening on a world I often do not see, have also inspired this book. It is a testament to my strenuous yet frequently unsuccessful effort to see the world through their eyes. I often think of Hermia's eloquent complaint, 'I would my father look'd but with my eyes.'[44] It is impossible, and perhaps undesirable, that people should look with each other's eyes, as I explain in the first chapter. We widely agree that many of the material and possibly even the ethical benefits of modernity derive from the irreducibility of multiple perspectives.

Although Aristotle listed spectacle as the least important component of tragic drama, the Greek term for theatre itself, as Shannon Jackson remarks, not only emphasizes 'the spectacular qualities of a thing beheld as well as a vision-based locus of reception and interpretation,' but also resists attempts to delineate it as a 'research object.'[45] Michael Fried has suggested that theatre is that which lies *between* the arts, and even that theatre is the 'negation of art' because it is concerned not with the art itself, the *thingness* of art, but with the circumstances or situation in which the beholder encounters the work.[46] His scepticism, expressed in the argument that theatre is a dubious ground for seeing things, has been immensely productive, yet it also contains blind spots that I will consider in my chapter on Samuel Beckett's *spectres du noir*. The words 'theatre' and 'theory' are derived from the same Greek root (θέα, *thea*, for viewing), and theatrical interpretation by performers, spectators, and historians is inherently speculative. In theatre studies this perception has led to a curious suspicion of the *thingness* of language without which interpretations of the things we see would be impossible.

Though concerned with the metaphysical and the theoretical, my project aims pragmatically to historicize a spirit that is not monolithic but multiple. Theatrical ghosts (a redundant phrase) challenge, subvert, and reinforce notions of inside/outside, subject/object, self/other, and material/spiritual in specific forms of theatre and drama. *Seeing Things* builds on work that charts the interaction between theatre and other cultural forms including philosophy and natural science, literature, painting, and movies. Shaped by the tradition inherited from the Greeks, I am preoccupied with the limitations of a visual register. Aristotle's valuation of spectacle as mere visual adornment to the tragedian's poetic art was already implied by the dramatic character King Oedipus, who represents the painful vulnerability of eyes even among the most perspicacious.

This book collects essays that, together, offer a historical narrative that traces changing relationships between viewers and the things viewed, starting with an early modern culture of gift-giving and a neo-Platonic rhetoric of love and sight. It then shifts its focus to the nineteenth century and Romantic ways of visualizing Hamlet's Ghost, before turning to Samuel Beckett's reaction against Romantic idealism and a post–Second World War disillusionment with spiritual modes of vision. The final chapter turns to the contemporary technology of digital animation and Pixar's self-reflexive take on visual reproduction in the absence of concrete things and the relation of these strategies of visual representation to Disney's marketing strategies. Pixar's toys represent a spiritual experience in the sense that something infinite emerges from the human-made or (supposedly) concrete; the toys' story is intricately interwoven both with a figuration of death and return and with the spirit of capitalism. In each of these instances, *Seeing Things* aims to illustrate practices, technologies, and theories of vision that organize discrete fields of experience.

Shakespeare's plays assume that there is a kind of knowledge that is inseparable from theatrical performance and that it is both ethical and metaphysical. These assumptions are informed by the tradition of classical humanism that shaped the thinking of his day. Plato's *Symposium*, which proposes that 'sight is midway between intellect and touch,' its translation in the Renaissance, and its interpretation over the ages, sets the stage for this study of *A Midsummer Night's Dream*, by providing an enduring configuration of terms and thematic concerns: of parents and offspring, of love and knowledge, of passion and reason, of the commensurable and the infinite. My first chapter draws on neoclassical theories of love and knowledge with which Shakespeare was familiar. It shows that the spirit of generosity enables one to see, to know, and to understand in ways that are not always quantifiable in the nature of things. It explains, in short, the relationship the play emphasizes between showing and knowing.

Chapter 2, 'Visualizing Hamlet's Ghost,' addresses a key problem for the drama since Shakespeare, namely, how to represent human interiority on the stage. Understanding what is meant by interiority is a historical problem, and in this chapter I describe the ways in which German and British Romantics become re-invested in notions of the spirit and quasi-theological ways of thinking that lead to a new way of imagining the relation of subject to object and the location of truth. The problem of the modern is the problem of seeing ourselves in transition, *becoming* rather than *being*, for what we transition *to* is a new way of seeing. This historic-epistemological transition is vitally related to changes in the concept of vision. In this context, *Hamlet*, with emphasis on the figure of the Ghost and on Hamlet's imagination, becomes a central *Romantic* text. I trace a genealogy that begins with Romantic interpretations of *Hamlet* and evolves in a dialogue, winding its way from Goethe to Ibsen to Wilde, which draws upon dramatic structures and terms, images, and even characters, taken from Shakespeare.

Samuel Beckett rejects speculative theories of human interiority. Beckett treats depth (in spatial, psychological, and metaphysical terms) as an illusion and employs the trope of flatness to expose the human impulse to project an invisible reality. Chapter 3, 'Samuel Beckett's *spectres du noir*,' shows that there is a relationship between physical and metaphysical flatness in Beckett's thought and, thus, paradoxically between flatness and *spectres*. The latter are introduced in Beckett's art criticism, but his work is pervaded by the words 'spirit,' 'soul,' and 'ghost.' Flatness and the problem of ghosts are not only metaphors but also crucial aspects of form in painting and other arts that make use of surfaces. So this chapter focuses on the medium of film and Beckett's art criticism. Film's important relationships to dramatic enactment in theatre and to the pictorial realism of photography extend debates about representation that are endemic to each. In his own venture into the medium, *Film*, Beckett pushes the figurative and literal flatness of the image to a breaking point in every sense. I understand Beckett's exploration of flatness in relation to Romantic theories of perception, the twentieth-century phenomenological tradition, post-war art criticism (and modernist reactions to the theory that art has an essence to disclose), as well as to media relationships Beckett chose as sites of investigation and his radical Protestant iconoclasm.

In the final chapter, 'The Spirit of Toys,' I turn to commodity fetishism. *Toy Story 2* enacts a fantasy of continual resurrection both in the games of an individual child and in the processes of production and marketing. 'The overriding desire of most children,' writes Baudelaire, 'is to get at and see the soul of their toys.'[47] We might say that Disney has enthusiastically adopted this poetic observation as a marketing slogan. The digitally animated *Toy Story* movies, the third of which was released in the summer of 2010, are deeply invested, thematically and financially, in the mortality of toys. Buzz Lightyear expresses the toys' metaphysical dimension in his famous slogan, 'To infinity and beyond!' The toy offers a vision of space that reflects digital media's own capacity to reproduce, and it serves as a challenge to older ways of understanding what it means to see *things* in material terms. Life and death are inseparable from the medium in which they are represented. The material of which these toys are supposedly made (they are, in fact, composed only of pixels and light) acquires anthropomorphic features from the supposed humanity of the owners. Their putative humanity is a prosthetic extension or projection.

The supersensible idiom of ghosts, souls, and spirits pervades this wide-ranging study but raises different questions in each case. It illuminates the modern problem of representing what is inside of us. Drawing on art from roughly 1600 to 2010, the book hinges on the nineteenth century, when developments of new visual technologies coincided with an epoch-making shift in the formation of historical consciousness that had begun in Shakespeare's day. The intensified awareness of seeing things in history was manifested in a wide range of literary, philosophical, and historiographical writings as an obsession with the idea of rebirth, recurrence, and the *revenant*. Kierkegaard's *Repetition* (*Gjentagelsen*), Burckhardt's invention of the Renaissance (in *Kultur der Renaissance in Italien*), Tolstoy's *Resurrection* (*Voskresenie*), Ibsen's *Ghosts* (*Gengangere*), Nietzsche's idea of eternal recurrence in *The Gay Science*, and many other works in the same spirit prompt us to rethink history and, in particular, our methods of literary-historical scholarship.[48] Offering close readings of popular and canonical texts, from *A Midsummer Night's Dream* to *Toy Story*, this book aims to provide a fresh and surprising history of things. An analysis of both material culture and aesthetic theory, it asks questions about efforts to observe, measure, exchange, and even capitalize the spirit. The notion of seeing across the modern period is inseparable from concrete constructions of subjectivity and desire. Spirits make scenes. They both epitomize the spectacular nature of the theatre and symbolize a structure of longing. Whether trapped in purgatory or a child's room, Hamlet's father, Jacob Marley, Sheriff Woody, and Buzz Lightyear lack freedom yet cannot be stayed. Things of nothing, they represent both the collapse and the return of the physical, as well as the temporality of vision, the imperfection of the senses, and the irrepressible power of human imagination.

# 1 A Spirit of Giving in *A Midsummer Night's Dream*

How I wish, said Socrates, taking his place as he was desired, that wisdom could be infused through the medium of touch, out of the full into the empty man ... For you would have filled me full of gifts of wisdom, plenteous and fair, in comparison of which my own is of a very mean and questionable sort, no better than a dream.

Plato, *The Symposium*

The history of drama in modernity is bound up with continual, and increasingly intense, negotiations between the self and the concrete, external world of objects. In the early modern context of *A Midsummer Night's Dream*, *things* serve as visible material tokens of feeling, objects through which spiritual and earthly goods are exchanged and conveyed. The vexation of Egeus in the first scene of *A Midsummer Night's Dream* is expressed in a list of those items that Lysander has given to his daughter: 'bracelets of thy hair, rings, gauds, conceits, / Knacks, trifles, nosegays, sweetmeats' (1.1.33–4). The objects in themselves are insignificant or, at least, interchangeable, homogeneous in value, and to those who consider passionate love for another person qualitatively special and hence incommensurable, such a list of 'knacks' and 'trifles' may appear trivializing if not degrading. But the angry father considers the objects to be messengers of strong prevailment. And the speech introduces a crucial theme, that of giving and taking, and associates the play's most prominent figure of fatherhood (and only biological parent) not simply with a rigid and old-fashioned rule of law but also with stinginess. In the face of the parent's example, the child too refuses to be generous. 'My soul *consents not to give* sovereignty,' Hermia says. Everyone begins the play more interested in taking than in giving.

The spirit of generosity is deeply related to a capacity for sympathy and specifically to the way in which a sympathetic disposition enables one to see, to know, and to understand. The importance of sympathetic understanding is introduced when Hermia says simply and poignantly, 'I would my father look'd but with my eyes' (1.1.56). Yet sympathetic understanding and generosity cannot be reduced simply to looking with another's eyes, and the play represents an extremely complex and richly dialectical ethical reality, one that privileges neither the perspective of Egeus nor that of Hermia. The irony of Hermia's wish is exposed in the radically changeable (irrational and manipulable) nature of young lovers' eyes. Later in the same scene, Helena goes so far as to say, 'Love looks not with the eyes but with the mind' (1.1.234). It would be absurd to imagine that anyone, let alone Egeus, *ought* to look with Hermia's eyes, much as she wishes it. As Marsilio Ficino wrote in a text Shakespeare was likely to have known, *Commentary on Plato's Symposium on Love* (c. 1474), 'Sight is midway between intellect and touch; hence the soul of the lover is always being pulled in opposite directions, and thrown alternately backwards and forwards.'[1]

A sympathetic understanding does not require direct identification. As the Scottish philosopher Adam Smith wrote a century and a half later: 'The compassion of the spectator must arise ... from the consideration of what he himself would feel if he was reduced to the same unhappy situation, and ... was at the same time able to regard it with his present judgment.'[2] For Smith, whose economic and moral thought defines and extends the socio-economic concerns beginning to arise in early modern Europe, the loss of reason is the most dreadful calamity that can happen to a person. From *A Midsummer Night's Dream* to *Timon of Athens*, Shakespeare's dramas continually interrogate a tension between the impulse towards spontaneous generosity and rational (often proto-capitalist) considerations. The former is not rational in itself, and so, in Smith's view, is always already removed from marketplace considerations. An interest in the happiness of others gives happiness to a spectator, Smith notes, 'though he derives nothing from it, except the pleasure of seeing it.'[3] The gifts of a lover such as Lysander are, of course, not given in this spirit. Like all lovers, he expects a return. He gives because he wants (i.e., lacks) love. To render sympathy, that combination of feeling and judgment, is to imagine not a relationship of lovers (or at least not the kind of lovers we find in this play) but a relation of spectator to actor. It is no mere coincidence that, for the eighteenth-century theorists of sympathy, theatre is a central metaphor.

To be magnanimous is to give only when one has imagined the position of the one to whom one gives, to allow for various forms of reception, and to grant that to which one gives birth a life of its own. The critical, like the poetic imagination, 'gives to airy nothing a local habitation and a name' (5.1.16). And the verb *to give* accumulates power over the course of the play. A seemingly more generous Theseus explains in the end that the onstage audience will be kinder 'to give' the rude mechanicals 'thanks for nothing' (5.1.89). The play itself, as Philostrate tells Theseus, is 'nothing, nothing in the world; / Unless you can find sport in their intents, / Extremely stretched and conn'd with cruel pains, / To do you service' (5.1.78–81). But what the actors themselves have given is only nothing in that richly complex sense of the word that Shakespeare explores most notably in *Hamlet*. It is a *thing of nothing*. After all, the rude mechanicals are those who appear to have least to give. Yet in giving a performance they give most of themselves. There is an important truth in the Prologue's remark, 'By their show, / You shall know all that you are like to know' (5.1.116–17).

In short, this chapter assumes that there is a kind of knowledge that is accessible through dialogue and inseparable from a particular structure of theatrical performance, that such a structure has analogies in the classroom, and that the knowledge in question is both ethical and metaphysical. These assumptions are inseparable from the tradition of classical humanism that deeply informed the thinking of Shakespeare's day. As Oscar Wilde imagines, through his own portrayal of passion and intellectual generosity in 'The Portrait of Mr W.H.,' one can discover in Shakespeare's plays an extension of Plato's rich meditations on creativity and love:

In 1492 appeared Marsilio Ficino's translation of the 'Symposium' of Plato, and his wonderful dialogue, of all the Platonic dialogues perhaps the most perfect, as it is the most poetical, began to exercise a strange influence over men, and to colour their words and thoughts, and manner of living . . . In the curious analogies it draws between intellectual enthusiasm and the physical passion of love, in its dream of the incarnation of the idea in a beautiful and living form, and of a real spiritual conception with a travail and a bringing to birth, there was something that fascinated the poets and scholars of the sixteenth century. Shakespeare, certainly, was fascinated by it, and had read the dialogue . . . Beauty is the goddess who presides over birth, and draws into the light of day the dim conceptions of the soul.[4]

Plato's *Symposium* provides a foundation for the present chapter not simply on account of Wilde's brilliant (yet coyly fictional) hypothesis about Shakespeare's debt to the dialogue, nor because of the numerous figural coincidences between it and *A Midsummer Night's Dream*. In *The Symposium*, Pausanias discusses the relationship of love to tyranny and notes the complete unreliability of the lover's oath. Eryximachus, the physician, talks about the universal quality of love, whose empire includes plants and animals, and claims that the wantonness of an overbearing love can affect the seasons and is 'a great injurer and destroyer, and is the source of pestilence.'[5] Rather than being interested in noting parallels, I am drawn to *The Symposium* in this case because it presents us, and perhaps presented Shakespeare, with an enduring configuration of terms and thematic concerns. These include relations of old and young, of parents and offspring both biological and philosophical, of love and knowledge, of passion and reason, of homogeneity and distinction, of the commensurable and the infinite, of pedagogy and generosity.

As Martha Nussbaum writes, '*The Symposium* recognizes, and shows, that human beings often lead disorderly and unsatisfactory lives because of the extent to which they are motivated by passionate love.'[6] But, she goes on, the dialogue offers a 'particular kind of teaching about the objects of love' whereby the lover begins to see a similarity between the value of a love object and other comparable values. Then, 'he *decides* that it is *prudent* to consider these related beauties to be "one and the same," that is, not just qualitatively close, but qualitatively homogenous, interchangeable instances of some one inclusive value.'[7] Claudius gives Hamlet just such 'prudent' advice when he identifies Hamlet's excessive grief/love for his father as irrational, disorderly, and more than usually unhappy. For Hamlet to single out his father as more deserving of such emotion than other fathers is 'To reason most absurd, whose common theme / Is death of fathers' (1.2.103–5). It little matters that Claudius may have ulterior motives. *King Lear* also begins with the problem of measuring love, which unfolds with the visual metaphor of the map. Lear assumes that love is measurable and plans to make gifts accordingly. And so does Cordelia. She works fractions on love. But the process is corrupted when, for instance, Goneril tells her father, 'Sir, I love you more than words can wield the matter' (1.1.55). In short, both 'good' and 'bad' characters in Shakespeare assume that love can be measured, just as both 'good' and 'bad' characters assume that love is incommensurable. As *King Lear* makes plain, the difficulty of measuring love is directly related to faulty, that is, human, vision. Lear's 'darker purpose,' to divide his kingdom, turns blacker than planned. He banishes first Cordelia from his sight and then Kent, who has 'Lov'd [him] as my father.' 'Out of my sight!' Lear exclaims. To which Kent replies, 'See better, Lear' (1.1.36, 157–8). To see better is to take a more careful measurement of love, not to accept, as the wicked daughters propose, that it is incommensurable. What is at stake in *A Midsummer Night's Dream* is another version of the problem of the commensurability of love that arises when individuals perceive heterogeneity and when irrationality (which depends upon the perception of heterogeneity) characterizes their behaviour. When Bottom says, 'reason and love keep little company together nowadays,' he implies that they are not necessarily incompatible (3.2.143–4).

When we say that a value (of love or of grief) is commensurable, we mean that it can be measured by a common standard, known, and managed (in emotional and financial senses – not only controlled but also directed). It enters into an economy of exchange, though not necessarily market, or capitalist, exchange. During the rise of capitalism, however, as Annette Weiner comments, 'the give and take of reciprocity took on an almost magical, sacred power among Western economists.'[8] Marx's critique of 'the fetishism of the commodity' in capitalism, which depends on the observation that various objects exchanged in the capitalist marketplace assume homogeneous value, may in this context be regarded also as a response to neo-Platonic, idealist metaphysics. 'A commodity appears at first sight an extremely obvious, trivial thing,' Marx comments. But, he adds playfully, 'its analysis brings out that it is a very strange thing, abounding in metaphysical subtleties and theological niceties.'[9] Marx perceives that products of labour are not special *as objects* when exchanged on the market. 'It is only by being exchanged,' he writes, 'that the products of labour acquire a socially uniform objectivity of values, which is distinct from their sensuously varied objectivity as articles of utility.'[10] Imagining gifts as Marx imagines commodities, Marcel Mauss argues that in pre-capitalist societies things-as-gifts are not 'indifferent things' but take on a life of their own.[11] Mauss assumes, like Marx, that gifts (commodities) represent social relationships. Commodities and gifts can assume symbolic, mystical, pseudo-metaphysical, and thus incommensurable value when they are removed from the marketplace. Socrates' argument in *The Symposium*, by contrast, assumes an absolute commensurability of value.

Shakespeare's plays set these positions in dialogue with each other. In *Twelfth Night*, Olivia quips glibly that her beauty can be 'inventoried' (1.5.246). While she may be facetious, in plays and sonnets Shakespeare commonly examines just what, if anything, the objects of love add up to. In this particular case Viola replies that in spite of Olivia's sarcasm and pride, Orsino's love for her could, in fact, be 'recompens'd, though you were crowned the nonpareil of beauty' (1.5.252–3). This form of knowing is specific and limiting. It is opposed to the Dionysian vitality of Sir Toby Belch, who will not 'confine [himself] within the modest limits of order' (1.3.8–9). And the problem of defining the limits of desire assumes a special resonance when considered in light of the entrepreneurial energy and acquisitive spirit of English merchants and adventurers in the Renaissance.

Irrational desire depends upon the perception of difference, of qualitative heterogeneity. It is precisely this *impression* of heterogeneity *in their own eyes* that distinguishes the lovers in *A Midsummer Night's Dream* from each other. As students commonly remark, it is difficult to tell the young Athenians apart. 'Through Athens,' Helena remarks, 'I am thought as fair as she [Hermia].' But 'Things base and vile, holding no quantity, / Love can transpose to form and dignity' (1.1.233–4). Without being a lover, that is, overcome by a desire to possess, one cannot perceive qualitative difference. On the other hand, without perceiving difference, one will not be overcome by desire. Which comes first, passionate desire or the perception of difference? Many critics have recognized in the play an irresolvable dialecticalism. Louis Montrose has written of the double sense of creation within the play: *A Midsummer Night's Dream* 'creates the culture by which it is created, shapes the fantasies by which it is shaped, begets that by which it is begotten.'[12]

As for seeing what is different between these lovers, Puck's failure to see what is special in them as individuals is, of course, the central twist of the plot. Lysander and Demetrius are not even distinguishable by their 'Athenian garments.' The former is regarded by Puck simply as 'the youth . . . / Pleading for a lover's fee.' And Puck's homogenizing claim, 'what fools these mortals be,' speaks directly to the ethical difference between himself and them. But would anyone say that Puck is ethically superior to the lovers whom he manipulates? 'Those things do best please me,' he says, 'That befall prepost'rously' (3.2.112–13, 115, 120–1). To imagine the commensurability of love is clearly not altogether to the good. To limit the spirit of love by assuming material equivalence, as Shylock appears to equate his daughter and his ducats, may damage love. To ask whether *A Midsummer Night's Dream* advocates the Socratic position that love ought to be commensurable and homogeneous or whether such a rational position degrades the spirit of love is to forget that it is not a treatise but an exceptionally self-conscious work of theatre. The play continually interrogates the interactions between actors and audience members.

The important question of measuring ethical values is central to the Western philosophical tradition, from Plato to Mill. Socrates asks if love is the love of something or of nothing? From the prophetess Diotima, he learns that love is not itself *a* good but an aspiration toward *the* good. Bertolt Brecht would later exploit a similar pun in German, focusing on the figure of the prostitute who sells 'love' as a 'good,' not just good but the goods, in *Die Ware Liebe* (the good [commodity] love), which became *Der gute Mensch von Sezuan* (the good person of Sezuan).[13] And if, since ancient Rome, actors have been identified with prostitutes, it is partly a sign of how their occupation combines the roles of servant and lover, both of whom give but expect something in return. Yet the question of love's commensurability and the trope of giving are also historically specific. The giving of gifts in *A Midsummer Night's Dream*, as elsewhere in Shakespeare, must be understood in the context of early modern economics, the growing importance of capital and the anxiety it produced. John Donne speaks of bargaining with the 'Usurious God of Love' in 'Love's Usury,' and in 'Lovers infinitenesse' the poet is torn between whether love can be purchased or given. This tension is also informed by a Christian (as opposed to, say, a Pythagorean) rhetoric of incarnation and redemption (also both a theological and economic term commonly employed by Donne).

Mercantilism, according to which accumulation is associated with paternalistic authority, and Christian imperialism are, in *A Midsummer Night's Dream*, perhaps even more significant than anxiety about capital as aspects of a developing economy of exchange that inform changing personal relations. As Stephen Greenblatt has written, 'The whole achievement of the discourse of Christian imperialism is to represent desires as *convertible* and in a constant process of exchange.'[14] This logic accounts for the rhetorical paradoxes in Columbus's encounter with the Indians whereby he imagines that taking absolute possession is at the same time to make an absolute gift. It is a similar absoluteness of both generosity and taking possession that characterizes Titania's treatment of another Indian princess, the nameless and now dead mother who (like Lysander to Hermia) gained her love by fetching trifles. Titania's keeping of the child is paradoxically an act of both possessiveness and generosity. Titania lovingly recalls how the woman would 'fetch me trifles, and return again, / As from a voyage, rich with merchandise' (2.1.133–4).

The spontaneous generosity exhibited by the vot'ress of her order is not the same as Titania's sense of responsibility. Greenblatt describes an almost identical disparity in terms of generosity in the encounter of the Spanish and the inhabitants of the New World:

> The spirit of gift-giving, as Columbus understands it, is not reciprocal: the Indians give out of an unconstrained openness of heart that is a marvel; the Spanish in return give out of a sense of what is right, a sense of obligation bound up with the conviction that the Indians have *already* become the Christian subjects of the sovereigns of Castile.[15]

This sort of romantic imagining of the Indian was most influentially articulated in the sixteenth century by Montaigne, who regarded New World peoples as 'close to their original simplicity' and 'governed by natural laws.' These natural and disinterested people, according to Montaigne, 'are still at the happy stage of desiring no more than their simple appetites demand,' and the women are immune to jealousy.[16] Titania's sense of obligation to her Indian vot'ress, on the other hand, cannot be attributed to sisterly devotion. Theirs is not a relationship, as Montrose suggests, analogous to the intimate bond between Hermia and Helena.[17] The very terms, 'a vot'ress of my order,' suggest that the Indian maid is not a kindly friend or helper involved in reciprocal exchange but a devotee bound up by vows to live a life of religious worship or service; she is a mortal and Titania a god. The Europeans imagined themselves in just such a relation to the inhabitants of the New World. And from Puck we have learned that, in fact, even after the mother's death the child was not parentless because the lovely boy was 'stolen from an Indian king' (1.2.22). This boy, who may be given or withheld by the fairy queen and king, is a human commodity of empire. As Greenblatt puts it, 'The conversion of commodities into gold slides liquidly into the conversion and hence salvation of souls.'[18] It is with precisely this paradoxical rhetoric of taking and giving that Theseus first addresses his own New World princess in *A Midsummer Night's Dream*.[19] To Hippolyta, Queen of the Amazons, he says, 'I woo'd thee with my sword, / And won thy love doing thee injuries,' to which she remains, significantly, silent (1.1.16–17).

Consummated love implies possession, but it is possession of a paradoxical sort. As Helena remarks, 'I have found Demetrius like a jewel / Mine own, and yet not mine own' (4.1.192–3). It is not difficult to hear in this rhetoric that of European adventurers confronted by the riches of the rest of the world. But it is qualified here by the important sense that Socrates addresses at length in *The Symposium*, that to love is to have not: 'He who desires something is in want of something.'[20] Love, always caught between having and wanting, is according to a Greek parable the child of Plenty and Poverty. If to love is to want, once you've got love, what do you have? The answer, suggests Diotima through Socrates, is that homogeneous value *the good*. However, the consummation of love in the characteristic idiom of the Renaissance is to die. We speak of love and of generosity, therefore, not just in material terms but as *spirit* because to do so implies a structure of mediation, even of liminality.

In *The Symposium* Socrates reports that the prophetess Diotima speaks of this betweenness as an operation between men and gods. That is the basis for defining love in terms of both the transaction of giving (men give prayers and sacrifices to the gods, and the gods give commands and rewards to men) and of spirit.

> 'What then is love?' I asked; 'Is he mortal?' 'No.' 'What then?' 'As in the former instance, he is neither mortal nor immortal, but *in a mean between them.*' What is he, then Diotima?' 'He is a great spirit (δαίμων), and like all that is spiritual he is intermediate between the divine and the mortal.' 'And what is the nature of this spiritual power?' I said. 'This is the power,' she said, 'which interprets and conveys to the gods the prayers and sacrifices of men, and to men the commands and rewards of the gods.'[21]

Love, Diotima convinces Socrates, is neither fair nor good, but neither is it foul or evil. Love 'spans the chasm which divides [men and gods], and in this all is bound together.' The chasm is a metaphor that Shakespeare expands in Theseus's famous speech about the poet and the lover, who 'glance from heaven to earth, from earth to heaven' and whose imaginations body forth the 'forms of things unknown' (5.1.14–15). The power of love is *poetic*, in the Greek sense of the term (*to make*), a power 'which interprets and conveys'; it is creative. As Ficino comments, 'It was for this reason that Diotima ... called love a *daemon*. Because, just as the daemons are midway between heavenly things and earthly things, so love occupies the middle ground between formlessness and form.'[22]

For Diotima, the understanding of love is not (exclusively) empirical or material but spiritual, largely because love itself is always a mean between two terms: good and evil, fair and foul, knowledge and ignorance, plenty and poverty, having and wanting, giving and taking. Love, though not itself good, she explains, desires possession of the good. In *A Midsummer Night's Dream* it is clear from the beginning that love is not inherently generous. On the contrary, love tends to be possessive, greedy, and exclusionary. When Helena first enters, she immediately proposes a gift with one crucial reservation: 'Were the world mine, Demetrius being bated, / The rest I'd give to be to you translated' (1.2.192–3). But the exception of Demetrius is the key point. And why would Helena give anything, let alone the world, to Hermia? The only object of such giving is to gain her one desire, a painful if understandable perversion of generosity. 'My legs,' laments the long-limbed Helena, 'can keep no pace with my desires.' Similarly, Titania's possessive love leads her to complain that Oberon has only turned up since Theseus is to be wedded to Hippolyta, 'To give their bed joy and prosperity' (3.2.445, 2.1.73). What can be wrong with exercising this generous impulse? The problem is that Titania is jealous and wants Oberon to give to no woman but herself. When giving must be governed by such rigid policies of exclusion it can hardly be said to be generous.

Generosity and Desire are here mutually constitutive or, in the language of literary theory, supplementary terms. And the opening scene of the play is quick to establish this playfully binary structure. Those who have most to give, the paternalistic Egeus and Theseus, are riven by selfish desire. Theseus declares that his 'desires' have become vexing rather than happy because he has had to wait so long to be given what he wants, his nuptial hour with Hippolyta. And who in his view is the stingy one, depriving him of pleasure? It is Nature herself refusing to give. The old moon keeps him waiting, 'Like to a step-dame or a dowager / Long withering out a young man's revenue.' He instructs Hermia to 'question your desires,' but does not question his own (1.1.5–6, 67, 126). As the older men exit, Egeus oddly declares that he follows Theseus not just with duty but also with 'desire.' They do not set a good example for their charges who are greedy for love. The figurative dowager, the moon of which Theseus complains, also finds a more concrete echo in the opening scene. This 'dowager / Of great revenue' is crucial to the plot, as Lysander explains to Hermia that his widow aunt who plans to give him everything has a place seven leagues from Athens where they can rendezvous.

What is especially striking in the references to dowagers and the dependence not only of Lysander but also of Theseus upon the 'will' of even a mythical woman is that the idea of an unmarried woman, possessing disposable property, according to English common law, would have been an anomaly. Who is a woman of power and great revenue who hath no child, whose home, secure from Athenian law, will protect the young and persecuted? It will not tax the imagination to suppose that one model for such a childless, powerful, and potentially generous woman is the ultimate patron of the Lord Chamberlain's Men, Queen Elizabeth herself. The paradoxical status of the female monarch in a patriarchal culture is rendered in starkest relief in the first scene of the play in terms of giving and waiting to be given. The ability of women to dispense gifts within a patrilineal system leads not only to the problematic question of ownership but also, as *The Symposium* shows, to the gendered nature of both love and generosity. One of the most remarkable features of that complex dialogue is that, deeply embedded within the Chinese boxes of narrative, it is the female Diotima, not the phallogocentric Socrates, who is the source of wisdom on this subject. In Shakespeare's social reality, the tension engendered by the paradoxical *need*, not just the expectation, for women (the moon, the dowager aunt, Titania, the Queen, Shakespeare's daughter Susanna Hall), who are commonly expected to *be given* (in marriage), to *give* to men is dramatic, for it embodies a vital conflict. 'The movements of persons and possessions through time and space,' writes Weiner, 'are bound by, and to, the temporality of birth and death as well as production and decay.' This temporal experience tends to challenge 'convictions that a woman's sexuality and her role in reproduction make her into a property that must be exchanged and controlled by men.'[23]

In 1596, when *A Midsummer Night's Dream* is supposed to have been written, Shakespeare's son, Hamnet, died. As Ann Rosalind Jones and Peter Stallybrass have shown, the famous provision in Shakespeare's own will by which he left his second-best bed to his wife belies the fact that his best bed would have gone to Hamnet if he had lived. But, they point out,

> given the absence of a male heir, the bed, together with the Stratford house itself, went to his daughter Susanna Hall and to 'her heirs forever' . . . More striking and unusual is the emphatic expression of the intent to take back the property from the female heirs and give it to the male heir. The will goes to extraordinary lengths to insist upon male inheritance.[24]

If *A Midsummer Night's Dream* is haunted by a stolen boy, it is also informed by the related problem of men giving to women who, it is hoped, will give (if not be given) back to men. This play and others by Shakespeare begin by assuming a rigidly closed social and legal structure within which only a specific form of giving literally *makes sense*. And the social construction of the very idea of generosity is a thread that binds together several plays that might otherwise seem formally and thematically diverse.

*Timon of Athens* begins with a scene that mirrors the opening of *A Midsummer Night's Dream* in just this way. An Old Athenian father, like Egeus, approaches Lord Timon to request help in the giving of his daughter:

> One daughter have I, no kin else,
> On whom I may confer what I have got.
> The maid is fair, a' th' youngest bride,
> And I have bred her at my dearest cost
> In qualities of the best. This man of thine
> Attempts her love. I prithee, noble lord,
> Join with me to forbid him her resort,
> Myself have spoke in vain.                    (1.1.122–9)

The father's anxiety is that he will lose control over his personal property, that it will no longer be his to give, that the very capacity of giving will be stolen from him by a female *will*. The daughter is dear in a financial sense; she can be inventoried. Her 'qualities of the best' are vague enough to be accessible to anyone with a like store of ducats. Timon solves the marital problem simply, recognizing that the father seeks a suitor for his daughter distinguished by, not quality, but quantity of love (i.e., money). He gives his servant the means to marry the old man's daughter.

In the end, the tragedy of Timon, whose very name (from the Greek *timos*) means 'value,' is a chiasmic reflection of the comedic resolution, with lovers' nuptials, of *A Midsummer Night's Dream*. The instigating problem of both plays is the relation between love and generosity. The action in both moves from Athens to the woods before returning to Athens. Ultimately, both show it is not what is or is not given that is important but the spirit in which it is given. As in *King Lear*, a parent can give his children an entire kingdom but not give well. If Timon's fall is tragic it is because, as he ruefully remarks, 'Unwisely, not ignobly have I given' (2.2.175). Timon, like so many of Shakespeare's lovers, gives 'trifles' of his love, but it is even such trifles that are his undoing. Shakespeare's Athenians are governed by self-interest. Timon naively supposes himself above marketplace considerations: 'I gave it [my love] freely ever, and there's none / Can truly say he gives if he receives.' And the angry bewilderment that he expresses once he realizes that he has behaved according to an entirely different set of economic assumptions than the rest of his society is extreme and self-destructive. 'Cut my heart in sums,' he laments, having learned that love itself is subject to calculation (1.2.10–11, 3.4.93). If Timon bears a resemblance to Theseus (even presiding over a feast at which appears a masque of Amazons), there is also a direct link to that nameless, spontaneously generous Indian vot'ress, who fetched trifles for Titania but died so far from Athens. After his fall Timon, disdaining humanity, digs for roots in the woods, and in one of the play's cruellest ironies, he discovers gold. But he is the anti-adventurer, not the conquistador but the conquered. Timon will never go back on his oath to abjure society. 'I am no idle votarist,' he declares (4.3.27).

Yet the misanthropy to which Timon descends upon losing everything, retreating to the woods, is an extreme and untenable position. The fact that *Timon of Athens* and *A Midsummer Night's Dream* are both set in the Athens of antiquity lends power and immediacy to the sense that the plays speak to each other. Alcibiades, the last character to enter the feast in *The Symposium*, also attends Timon's feast and remains one of his most faithful friends. Shakespeare, who would have learned of Alcibiades from Plutarch's *Lives* if not from *The Symposium*, would also have known that it was by Lysander, the Spartan commander, that this follower of Socrates, the general Alcibiades, was defeated at Notium in 406 BCE and at whose behest he was murdered two years later. If the figure of Alcibiades provides a convenient lynchpin for these three texts, he also enables this chapter to return to the pedagogical spirit of a generous theatrical performance and the complex material and imaginative relations between spectators and things. After Socrates concludes his stirring lesson in what Benjamin Jowett translates as 'the things of love' by saying that the mind's eye, informed by the animating spirit of love, will bring forth not mere images of beauty but realities, there is a tremendous knocking at the door. Arriving at the end of a long night, the drunk Alcibiades plops down and discovers himself seated next to the master. 'By Heracles,' Alcibiades exclaims, 'What is this? Here is Socrates always lying in wait for me, and always, as his way is, coming out at all sorts of unsuspected places.'[25] Socrates turns to Agathon and begs his protection. But Alcibiades crowns Socrates with ribands and declares that, if he is to join the party, for his part he will praise not Love but Socrates.

The appropriateness of this shift in subject, from Love to the figure of Socrates, in *The Symposium* may be discovered in the deep relationship between Love and the critical imagination. Once she has enabled Socrates to see that all men desire the good and that the possession of the good leads inevitably to happiness, Diotima explains that men only appear to love different things because one part of love is separated off and receives the name of the whole. In fact, 'the beauty in every form is one and the same!'[26] People tend to think in terms of different kinds of love, but, in fact, all forms of love are ultimately of that homogeneous value, the good. Shakespeare takes up this idea at the conclusion of *As You Like It*, when Rosalind reappears in her 'true' womanly form to her father, Duke Senior, and her lover, Orlando. Unlike Cordelia, who reserves half her love for her husband and half for her father, she has no trouble giving herself wholly as both daughter and bride, saying to each: 'To you I give myself, for I am yours,' to which each replies in turn: 'If there be truth in sight, you are my daughter,' and 'If there be truth in sight, you are my Rosalind' (5.4.116–20). True love – the discovery of truth in sight – is an intellectual activity, a shaping quality of vision that Diotima in the *Symposium* likens to poetry or making, for love is not only of beauty but also of the birth of beauty. It is through the birth of beautiful children and of art that 'the mortal nature is seeking as far as is possible to be everlasting and immortal' or, in other words, through which humanity realizes itself. As Jowett eloquently summarizes the dialogue:

> Love is another aspect of philosophy. The same want in the human soul which is satisfied in the vulgar by the procreation of children, may become the highest aspiration of intellectual desire . . . the absorption and annihilation of all other loves and desires in the love of knowledge . . . To most men reason and passion appear to be antagonistic both in idea and fact . . . Yet this 'passion of the reason' is the theme of the Symposium of Plato.[27]

*A Midsummer Night's Dream* concludes with speeches on making art ('First, rehearse your song by rote, / To each word a warbling note') and beautiful children ('And the blots of Nature's hand / Shall not in their issue stand') before Puck delivers his famous, final address to the audience. Underscoring the relations between culture and nature, intellectual creativity and procreation, love and generosity, they evoke and reply to the concerns of Egeus's early speech on love-tokens.

In opening this chapter with the list of items that Lysander is alleged to have given Hermia, I was not precisely accurate, for the first 'love-token' of which Egeus complains is not a concrete object but poetry. 'Thou hast given her rhymes,' he begins, as if art tops all 'love-tokens,' as in this play it does. Audaciously, Lysander has 'sung' to his lady. And this kind of 'giving,' Egeus explains in a peculiar twist, is a form of taking, even of stealing:

> Thou hast by moonlight at her window sung
> With feigning voice verses of feigning love,
> And stol'n the impression of her fantasy,
> With bracelets of thy hair, rings, gauds, conceits,
> Knacks, trifles, nosegays, sweetmeats – messengers
> Of strong prevailment in unhardened youth.          (1.1.28–35)

The *gauds* themselves are not substantial but are valuable, like verses, largely for the spirit in which they are given and received. The word itself comes from the Latin *gaudere* (to delight in), signifying the importance of the temporal experience of the object rather than the thing itself. Indicating the lack of special value in the gauds themselves at the end of the play, Demetrius comments, on awakening to a renewed love of Helena, that his 'melted' love to Hermia now seems as 'the remembrance of an idle *gaud*' (4.1.167). Here, perhaps anticipating the 'remembrances' that Ophelia 're-delivers' to Hamlet, the fact that the love tokens amount to nothing in themselves is enabling rather than disabling. They are the transitory forms through which an idealist spirit or essence of love (or beauty or the good) has been inventoried and expressed.

In the same sense, the play of the rude mechanicals in the otherwise anticlimactic fifth act brings the central trope of giving trifles to a climax that enables the audience of lovers to manifest their love by giving trifles ('thanks for nothing,' i.e., applause) in return. 'The best in this kind are but shadows; and the worst are no worse, if imagination amend them,' says Theseus, who, like Hamlet, now appreciates the value of giving to players who give so little of substance in return (5.1.211–12). Hamlet's instinctive appreciation of the importance of being generous to actors is one of his most attractive and ennobling traits. Actors, he knows, like the ghost of his father, give everything and nothing, something of themselves but a thing upon which one cannot lay a hand. Generosity to the player, one hopes, will be repaid by generosity in kind. To Polonius, who plans to use the players according to their desert, Hamlet explains, 'The less they deserve, the more merit is in your bounty' (2.2.536).

*A Midsummer Night's Dream*, which begins with a denunciation of giving, ends with a plea to be generous to 'these visions' and a double image of giving. Puck speaks these last lines: 'Give me your hands, if we be friends, / And Robin shall restore amends' (5.1.426–7). To give one's hands is to give nothing, or at least to give what one also still retains. To be generous, to imagine without actually occupying other positions, to be critical but to refrain from censure, is the necessary basis for receiving gifts in turn. As Olivia instructs Malvolio in *Twelfth Night*, 'To be generous, guiltless, and of free disposition, is to take those things for bird-bolts that you deem cannon-balls' (1.5.90–3). Generosity informs perception. Yet the logic of *A Midsummer Night's Dream* extends further; the spirit of generosity expects a return but nothing more than a dream may yield. Alexander Leggatt writes in his chapter on this play: 'The audience has the most important role of all. It must, by its own response, give value to things that might otherwise be trivial. If it is to take the illusion of art as a kind of reality, then its perceptions must be, like those of a lover, generous to the point of irrationality.'[28] Though Leggatt encourages the spectator, like the lover, to succumb to a degree of irrationality in order to 'give value' to the players' performance, his own criticism is not irrational. Like the audience and the lover, the teacher-critic receives most when he is kindest, though what he gives be nothing greater than a dream. As Ficino wrote of Socrates: 'So the teacher is a helper rather than a master. That is why . . . Socrates declares he is the son of a mid-wife and most like a mid-wife in that he does not stuff knowledge into people when he teaches them, but rather elicits it, just as mid-wives deliver babies who have already been conceived.'[29] The helping teacher, like the lunatic, the lover, the poet, and the open-hearted parent, can see the good in nothing. But this neoclassical language of love and knowledge also assumes that each of us carries, somewhere within, an authentic self, a source of subjectivity and of art that is only waiting to be born and, thus, expressed. It is on this idealistic notion that modern visual culture focuses its most vital imaginative energies and radical disillusionments.

# 2   Visualizing Hamlet's Ghost: The Theatrical Spirit of Modern Subjectivity

*Hamlet*: Do you see nothing there?
*Queen*: Nothing at all, yet all that is I see.

*Hamlet* 3.4.136–7

Ineluctable modality of the visible: at least that if no more, thought through my eyes ... Shut your eyes and see.

James Joyce, *Ulysses*

Plays have always represented a reality that is invisible, whether psychological, biological, metaphysical, or theological. A key problem for the drama since Shakespeare has been to represent or express human interiority on the stage. Understanding what is meant by interiority, however, is also, more generally, a historical problem. The premise of this chapter is that a widespread re-imagining of the subject in the early decades of the nineteenth century is fundamental to what we think of today as the 'modern' drama. This period, often characterized as Romantic, sees a re-investment in notions of the spirit and quasi-theological ways of thinking, a new way of imagining the relation of subject to object and the location of truth. In the preface to his *Phenomenology of Mind* (*Phänomenologie des Geistes*, 1806), Hegel claims, 'Our age is a birth-time, and a period of transition. The spirit of man has broken with the old order of things ... In like manner the spirit of the time, growing quietly ripe for the new form it is to assume, disintegrates one fragment after another of the structure of its previous world.'[1] This transition is fundamentally related to changes in the concept of vision. In this context, *Hamlet*, with emphasis placed upon the figure of the Ghost and on Hamlet's imagination, becomes a central Romantic text. This chapter traces a genealogy that begins, therefore, not simply with *Hamlet* but with Romantic interpretations of *Hamlet* and evolves into a debate in which dramatic structures and terms, images, and even characters taken from *Hamlet* are represented in turn by artists such as Goethe, Ibsen, and Wilde. *Hamlet* is the crucial work through which Romantic audiences negotiated the dynamic relationship between modern subjectivity and the suddenly unstable experience of seeing things.

As everyone knows, the ghost of Hamlet's father first appears to sentinels on the ramparts of Elsinore. They are anticipating an action of some kind to be precipitated from *without*, but we learn after the Ghost's appearance that something is rotten *in* the state of Denmark. This rampart wall and the borders of the castle then become metaphors for the boundaries of the self which, as we are told repeatedly by characters in the play, has its own divisions between outer and inner, visible and invisible, the 'exterior [and] the inward man' (2.2.6). A key feature of what we understand as modern consciousness is that knowledge is authorized not by an external order, but, as Charles Taylor writes, that 'the certainty of clear and distinct perception is unconditional and self-generated.'[2] For Descartes, writing a few decades after Shakespeare, the division of body and spirit, outside and inside, becomes the key to self-sufficient certainty. But Descartes, like Hamlet, thinks of knowledge in terms of representation. The *cogito* is represented, that is, objectified, for the subject who recognizes himself (*ergo sum*). Descartes, too, thinks in terms of his 'mind's eye,' a phrase he commonly uses. And there are moments when, despite his confidence in rationality, Descartes seems haunted by a confusing world of images 'when I slightly relax my attention, my mind, finding its vision somewhat obscured and so to speak blinded by the images of sensible objects.'[3] The world of sensible objects enters and clouds the space of the mind.

Hegel's model of self-consciousness seeks to transcend (*aufheben*) the opposition between self and other, individual subject and nature, essence and appearance, by positing a unity of all things in the Spirit. This unity is the end of Hegel's dialectic of self-consciousness, as represented most famously in chapter 4 ('The Truth of Self-Certainty') of *The Phenomenology of Mind*. Hegel shows that consciousness requires consciousness of an other for self-consciousness; only when the other is recognized as identical with self is self-certainty achieved. But how or in what *form* is this other to be represented to the self? *The Phenomenology* itself suggests a bewildering array of forms through which the Spirit is manifest. Ultimately, as Taylor writes, 'the spirit which expresses itself in the external reality of nature comes to conscious expression in man.'[4] Significantly, for the Romantics, though not for Hegel, art comes to be regarded as the highest human activity. And the importance of an expressive rather than a mimetic or reflective notion of art is one thread that will run through theories of the drama from Coleridge to Wilde. For Hegel art and drama in particular are vital in the process of self-realization. But if the work of art, instead of manifesting something visible beyond itself, constitutes itself as the locus of manifestation, where is *it* to be located? Hegel's Spirit exists simultaneously inside, outside, and in between. Karl Löwith remarks: 'What appealed to Goethe about Hegel was nothing less than the principle of his spiritual activity: mediation between self-being (*Selbstsein*) and being other (*Anderssein*).'[5]

In *Hamlet*, Shakespeare is faced with the problem of theatre, of literally making visible subjects and objects of knowledge. The Ghost's appearances (entrances and exits) across the boundaries of the stage are emblematic of that problem. The dichotomy between inside and outside is, of course, understood by Hamlet himself as a theatrical division between appearance and reality (he has 'that within which passes show' [1.2.85]), but his notion of playing (as opposed to being), seems to allow for no interior space; his metaphor is the mirror. Other characters represent variations on the problem of seeing/knowing. 'How should I your true love know / From another one?' sings Ophelia, signifying a basic epistemological problem of the theatre. Pragmatic Fortinbras 'makes mouths at the invisible event' (4.5.23–4, 4.4.50). The question for the modern self, however, will cease to be what is inside and what is outside, but what constitutes inside and what constitutes outside. In 1875 Edward Dowden writes: 'Things in their actual, phenomenal aspect flit before [Hamlet] as transitory, accidental and unreal. And the absolute truth of things is ... only, if at all ... to be attained in the *mind*.'[6]

More recently, David Hillman, cutting against the grain of most readings of *Hamlet* since the Romantics, argues that Shakespeare's plays are preoccupied with an imagination of the *visceral interior* of the human body.[7] For the Elizabethan sceptic the problem of other minds is a problem (the 'matter') of other bodies. What is especially curious in this provocative argument about Hamlet's search for material knowledge is its elision of the spirit, the Ghost as a ghost, who, after all, instructs Hamlet's 'soul' and epitomizes *betweenness*. Generally, modern interpreters have privileged the murkiness of Hamlet's inner life as a source of the play's complexity and power. Freud describes the play as an example of 'the secular advance of repression in the emotional life of mankind.'[8] But Freud's approach is hardly empirical; he analyses Hamlet's *in*action, his 'hesitations,' the *nothing* that he performs, eliding Hamlet's often contradictory investment in theatricality and his impulse to judge others based on superficial impressions. Jacques Lacan would later describe Freud's method as Cartesian: 'The question is – of what can one be certain? With this aim, the first thing to be done is to overcome that which connotes anything to do with the content of the unconscious . . . to overcome that which floats everywhere, that which marks, stains, spots the text of any dream interpretation – *I am not sure, I doubt.'*[9] Doubt is a sign that I think, and by virtue of thinking, I am. Hamlet himself doubts. Where does the ghost of his father come from? Freud's response: from the sources of his own desire. Lionel Trilling traces the root of the problem of finding 'one's own self' to *Hamlet*, noting that Freud 'took the first steps towards devising a laborious discipline of research to discover where it might be found.'[10] In fact, however, that self is never actually found within the limits of the play, and the emphasis placed by Trilling and Freud not just on the interiority of the self but on the interiority of the relationship between self and other is characteristic of critics since Coleridge.[11] For audiences since the Romantics a crucial assumption is that the 'within' is privileged in *Hamlet*.[12] Yet the unconscious, like the Ghost, appears paradoxically as an absence. How do we account for the gap between perception and representation? Remarkably, whether privileging the internal life of the character or the dramatic world that impinges on him, most interpretations of the drama have tended to skirt the representational apparatus of the theatre.

One of the better known exceptions to the preference for Hamlet's inner life is instructive for its polemical irony. For T.S. Eliot, 'The play is the primary problem, and Hamlet the character only secondarily.'[13] Eliot singles out two critics as exemplary of the creative but weak minds typically drawn to the character of Hamlet: Goethe and Coleridge. They see in Hamlet a 'vicarious existence for their own artistic realization.' Eliot complains that weak/creative critics, like them, ignore relevant historical facts, but he appears not to believe that criticism requires the same kind of historicizing. Instead, in the objective correlative, he advocates a hypostatic notion of the *spirit*. He also represents it in the morality-playish Tempters that objectify Thomas Becket's emotional and spiritual conflict in *Murder in the Cathedral*. As Eliot's essay implies, the notion that the world of *things* in *Hamlet* becomes intelligible *only* through analysis of Hamlet's mind is an ideological development of the late eighteenth and early nineteenth centuries. But Eliot seems purposely to ignore the importance of this implication, most explicitly in a figure like Prufrock, who is 'not Prince Hamlet, nor was meant to be' and whose mind operates 'as if a magic lantern threw the nerves in patterns on a screen.' The shift in critical emphasis, which has radical ramifications for dramaturgical structures, performances, and playwriting of what we consider the modern drama, is plainly derived from writings of the early nineteenth century that present radical new views on subjectivity and spiritual experience.

But how is such experience represented in visual terms? The soul or spirit of a character, like ghosts of the dead, frequently resists representation. Visibility thus obtains importance in terms of both form and content. In theatrical terms the problem of the visual defines the relation of spectator to spectacle. How is the action materially framed or marked off; that is, what does the audience agree to see and what not to see? What *can* be seen? A play, like a painting, declares its subject by marking its spatial limits. Shakespeare thematizes the problem of such visual markers in the theatre not only by having his ghost appear first on the borders of Elsinore but also by placing a number of spectators within the play itself, beginning with a few radically uncertain sentinels and a scholar in scene 1. The modern drama, with infinitely more supple technologies of lighting than Shakespeare possessed, is literally shaped by incomplete distinctions between light and dark and may play more or less self-reflexively with the fraught space between the visible and invisible. Dramatists were especially affected by the invention of the electric light bulb in 1879, but early-nineteenth-century theatres also had the resource of gas-lighting and mirrors. In Edwin Booth's famous production of *Hamlet*, 'the house lights (gas jets) were very much lowered, if not completely extinguished, so that in the Ghost scenes the nocturnal effects made their point ... By this subdued light the individuals on the stage seem as if but shadowed forth in outline, and even the two friends of Hamlet, who 'hold the watch tonight,' partake of the supernatural element which invests the whole scene.'[14] Significantly, phantasmagoria exhibitions achieved the height of their popularity in the first half of that century.

The second aspect of the problem of visibility (deeply related to the problem of defining the boundaries of the aesthetic object) is to establish the relation of subject or beholder to object. This problem is partly one of the theatre, and in the nineteenth century both new technologies and new theories of vision contributed to eroding the subject–object distinction.[15] In fact, Goethe begins his *Theory of Colours* (1810) with a discussion of colours that 'belong altogether, or in a great degree, to the *subject* – to the eye itself.'[16] These physiological colours that have previously been 'banished into the region of phantoms,' he claims, are the foundation of his whole doctrine. In *Hamlet* the first exchange between Hamlet and Horatio after the Ghost's initial appearance represents a momentary confusion of the bodily/spatial metaphor of seeing:

> *Hamlet*: ... My father – methinks I see my father.
> *Horatio*: Where, my lord?
> *Hamlet*: In my mind's eye, Horatio.                    (1.2.184–6)

Hamlet's vision cannot be literal; no physical image is apparent to any spectator, though the jumpy Horatio initially misinterprets the remark. A detailed record of Edmund Booth's *Hamlet* (1870) indicates how an actor might emphasize metaphorical seeing in these lines: '*In* (deep sound) my *mind's* (upward accent) eye, Horatio (rising inflection).'[17] But Horatio too had referred to the Ghost after its first appearance as 'a mote to trouble the mind's eye.' Horatio, like Hamlet, is a Wittenberg-educated philosopher, detached enough to be a surrogate for the audience. But Hamlet is no sceptic (he accepts news of the Ghost sighting at face value but doubts its meaning), while Horatio, more like later audiences, will find his assumptions about relations between the material and spiritual worlds severely tested by the Ghost.[18] The slippage in Hamlet and Horatio's dialogue, from metaphorical to literal and back to metaphorical seeing, touches upon the very nature or roots of the theatre, in the Greek *theatron*, or place of seeing. Do we still have theatre when the reality represented is physically unseen? And what is the relation of the Ghost to this notion of the theatrical?

Beginning with the act of watching and, then, the appearance of the spectre in act 1, scene 1, *Hamlet* is full of spectators and plays-within-the-play: observable actions, observable inaction, and the unobservable, the unverifiable (e.g., the method in Hamlet's madness) or the concealed (e.g., the spying and soon corpsed Polonius). Before *The Mousetrap* Hamlet tells Horatio, 'when thou *seest* that act afoot ... *Observe* my uncle' (3.2.78–80). Hamlet intends to make a judgment based upon how Claudius seems, though he himself, paradoxically (hypocritically?), knows not seems.[19] In the first exchange with Horatio, however, Hamlet straightens out the problem of his father's *appearance* quickly as he clearly asserts a distinction between a metaphor for thought and a concrete reality that exists in objectifiable form outside of the body.

The separation of vision from the body, of the mental image from the concrete reality, is a separation that *Hamlet* begins to interrogate. This separation is reconsidered with far-ranging consequences at the beginning of the nineteenth century. In Coleridge's view, 'Hamlet beheld external objects in the same way that a man (of vivid imagination) who shuts his eyes, sees what has previously made . . . an impression upon his . . . organs.'[20] A recognition of the deep relationship between the historical construction of vision and the history of subjectivity is key to defining the *modern* drama. 'Remember,' Oscar Wilde explained to a journalist in 1884, 'in Shakespeare's day ghosts were not shadowy, subjective conceptions, but beings of flesh and blood, only beings living on the other side of the border of life, and now and then permitted to break bounds.'[21]

In the decades following the French Revolution, as M.H. Abrams remarks, the commonly noted 'secularization of inherited theological ideas and ways of thinking' involved a reformulation of 'traditional concepts, schemes, and values which had been based on the relation of the Creator to his creature and creation.' God's relation to the universe was reformulated in terms of the 'prevailing two-term system of subject and object, ego and non-ego, the human mind or consciousness and its transactions with nature.'[22] The terra incognita of poetic exploration was no longer the heaven and hell of traditional Christian epic but the inner landscape of the human mind.[23] In *Sartor Resartus*, Thomas Carlyle represents a conservative reaction to the epistemological changes of the time in his deeply ironic depiction of the protagonist Teufelsdrökh: 'It is in his stupendous Section, headed *Natural Supernaturalism*, that the Professor first becomes a Seer . . . Worst of all, two quite mysterious, world-embracing Phantasms, Time and Space, have ever hovered round him, perplexing and bewildering: but with these also he now resolutely grapples, these also he rends asunder. In a word, he has looked fixedly on Existence, till, one after the other, its earthly hulls and garnitures have all melted away; and now, to his rapt vision, the interior celestial Holy-of-Holies lies disclosed.'[24] Borrowing Carlyle's phrase (*Natural Supernaturalism*), Abrams details, through examples in various literary genres and countries, a displacement of ancient problems and ways of thinking from a supernatural to a natural frame of reference.

To extend the terms of that thesis, the history of theatre and dramatic genres undergoes similar changes. Melodrama, for instance, a genre that flourishes in the decades following the French Revolution and persists to this day, represents, as Peter Brooks has written, 'both the urge toward resacralization and the impossibility of conceiving sacralization other than in personal terms.'[25] And melodrama shares aspects of the impulse to make the empirical stand for the transcendental with genres developed later in the century, including realism, expressionism, and symbolism. 'Clearly,' Strindberg writes provocatively in the 1890s, 'the spirits have taken to realism just as we human artists have.'[26] In short, the *modern* spirit runs through a gamut of genres.

Jonathan Crary describes the re-mapping of the visual field in the first decades of the nineteenth century in terms of historical 'figurations of an observer.' In contrast to 'the pervasive suppression of subjectivity in vision in seventeenth- and eighteenth-century thought,' Crary argues, such figurations 'in the early nineteenth century depended on the priority of models of subjective vision.'[27] The change that takes place from around 1810 to 1840 involves 'an uprooting of vision from the stable and fixed relations incarnated in the camera obscura,' as both a technology and a concept that was understood 'as an objective ground of visual truth.' Crary shows that 'what occurs is a new valuation of visual experience: it is given an unprecedented mobility and exchangeability, abstracted from any founding site or referent.'[28]

Of course, if Shakespeare seems to anticipate challenges to the camera obscura model described by Crary, one explanation is that performances of *Hamlet* (and most of Shakespeare's plays) happened simultaneously inside and outside, in the open-air theatre of the Globe; closet as well as battlement scenes were played upon the same boards with relatively little stage furniture to distinguish them. The plays were also performed in daylight; so spectators were required, imaginatively, to project the moonlight alluded to in night scenes, implicitly recognizing a spatial continuity between themselves and the characters on stage. The camera obscura, by contrast, as model and metaphor for the workings of human vision and for ways of knowing, requires a dark inner room in which are projected images from the sunlit world outside. In short, the camera obscura demands a sharp and legible delineation between light and dark.[29] Moreover, Shakespeare's plays manifest ample self-consciousness about the relation between vision and imagination. And yet, *Hamlet* reinscribes the epistemological structure implied by the camera obscura model, for Hamlet is an unhappy anomaly when it comes to problems of knowing. It is the very lack of a fixed reference point that so radically undermines Hamlet's confidence in his own judgment.

In one of his famous lectures 'on *Hamlet*' (1812), Coleridge articulates his own notion of the balance that the 'healthy' mind maintains 'between the impressions from outward objects and the inward operations of the intellect . . . In Hamlet this balance is disturbed: his thoughts and the images of his fancy, are far more vivid than his actual perceptions.'[30] Hamlet, like Coleridge himself, is an exceptional and unfortunate case. Yet, this conception, characteristic of the Romantic poets, of the shaping power of the imagination that interacts with the material world becomes increasingly prevalent in the nineteenth century. It is widely recognized that Romantic proclamations about art most commonly invoke the figurative language of overflow and expression. Wordsworth had defined poetic creativity in his 1802 preface to *Lyrical Ballads* as 'the spontaneous overflow of powerful feelings.' That overflow leads ultimately, in Wordsworth, to what seems like an erasure of the line between self and other, transforming him into a kind of ghost; he describes 'the Mind of Man' as 'My haunt, and the main region of my song.' The individual mind is 'limitless,' the 'line invisible / That parts the image from reality.'[31]

The most immediate relation between the mind and reality is considered to be visual. In *The World as Idea and Representation* (1819), for example, Schopenhauer ranks sight as the highest of the senses: 'its sphere is the most far reaching, and its receptivity and susceptibility the keenest. This is due to the fact that what stimulates it is an imponderable, in other words, something hardly corporeal, something quasi-spiritual.'[32] Schopenhauer too erases the subject–object correspondence, subverting distinctions between interior and exterior: 'Space itself is a form of our faculty of perception, in other words, a function of our brain. Therefore the "*outside us*" to which we refer objects on the occasion of the sensation of sight, itself resides inside our head, for there is its whole scene of action.'[33] This metaphor for perception simultaneously invokes theatrical terms and describes an experience that is fundamentally *internal*, within the body of the spectator.[34] Schopenhauer explicitly compares the general operation of vision to the experience of the spectator in the theatre who sees 'mountains, forest, sea,' though 'everything remains within the house.' *Things* exist in space '*only* insofar as we represent them.'[35]

Later treatments of optics would extend the notion that vision is spiritual and accentuate the liminality of the act of seeing. John Ruskin describes the optical lens itself as a threshold and the physical eye as a source of life: 'The power of the eye itself, as such, is *in* animation. You do not see *with* the lens of the eye. You see *through* it, and by means of that, but you see with the soul of the eye. Sight is an absolutely spiritual phenomenon, accurately, and only, to be so defined.'[36] Ruskin denies a fixed locus for the act of seeing, and his emphasis on prepositions indicates the importance of relations and movement. It also suggests an implicit critique of various aspects of materialism, and in this respect is continuous with nineteenth-century criticism on *Hamlet*. The American critic William Winter, for example, writes in 1863 that the role of Hamlet 'involves no sensual excitements, no sensuous delight, no gorgeousness of color, no celerity of movement. Its passion . . . is that of intense intellectuality.' This understanding of the character contributed to 'unsubstantial' representations of the Ghost.[37]

The terminology of eighteenth- and nineteenth-century vision studies obtains a remarkable degree of importance in writings on aesthetics and representation. Coleridge describes Hamlet's 'brooding over the world within him' in terms clearly taken from George Berkeley's 'Essay Towards a New Theory of Vision'; Berkeley coined the term 'outness': 'ideas of space, outness, and things placed at a distance [from the mind].'[38] Concerned more with the appearance of ideas in space than with.the experience of things distant from the mind, Coleridge writes: 'The prodigality of beautiful words . . . are as it were the half embodyings of thought, that make them more than Thought, give them an *outness*, a reality sui generis and yet retain their shadowy approach to the Images and movements within' (my emphasis).[39] Coleridge's 'and yet' marks a significant difference between himself and Berkeley, for whom the distinction between inner and outer was not 'shadowy.' Famous for his writer's block, Coleridge poignantly celebrates ideas, in the form of words, which can be projected outward. But, how can thought be only *half* embodied? Coleridge, paradoxically, betrays a historically new anxiety in the notion that even a half embodiment or 'outness' of thought may be greater than the image within, an argument that deconstructs both in the broader context of his oeuvre and in historical figurations of the subject–object relationship.

Significantly, Goethe's Wilhelm Meister, who is deeply identified with Hamlet, is first introduced to Shakespeare in terms of vision and isolation, through the metaphor of a new optical toy that represents a break from the camera obscura model of experience. 'You could not employ your time better,' Jarno tells Wilhelm, 'than by dissociating yourself from everything else and, in the solitude of your own room, peering into the kaleidoscope of this unknown world.'[40] Goethe not only shared Coleridge's love of *Hamlet*, but also was one of his generation's foremost theorists in the study of vision. In the opening pages of his *Theory of Colour*, as Crary has shown, Goethe adopts and transforms the camera obscura model to present a radically new model of vision as a corporeal phenomenon that subverts simple dichotomies of interior/exterior. The camera obscura operates as light is admitted into a dark room through a small circular hole that casts upon a wall of that interior an image of the outside world. Yet Goethe proposes a significant new experiment. 'Let the spectator ... fix his eyes on the bright circle ... The hole being then closed, let him look towards the darkest part of the room; a circular image will now be seen to float before him.'[41] Goethe describes a visual experience that occurs entirely in the interior of the body with no reference to an outer world. 'The closing off of the opening,' Crary explains, 'dissolves the distinction between inner and outer space on which the very functioning of the camera (as apparatus and paradigm) depended ... The coloured circles that seem to float, undulate, and undergo a sequence of chromatic transformations have no correlative either within or without the dark room.'[42] The image, writes Goethe, 'now belongs to the eye.' Illusion no longer has a status inferior to any other kind of optical experience; all optical experience is the experience of illusion, a highly personal, even private experience.

Indeed, Goethe's theory of the after-image is deeply related to his imagining of *Hamlet*'s Ghost, and *The Theory of Colour* may be read profitably in conjunction with the treatment of *Hamlet* in *Wilhelm Meister*. Goethe writes that 'images may remain on the retina in morbid affections of the eye' even longer than they do on healthy eyes, and 'this indicates extreme weakness of the organ, its inability to recover itself; while visions of persons or things which are the objects of love or aversion indicate the connexion between sense and thought.'[43] This morbidity of the eye is apparent in Wilhelm, who has, in a short time, both lost his own father and played a terrific Hamlet (especially in the ghost scenes), when, awakened at night, 'the image of the king in arms came before his heated imagination.'[44]

It is significant, therefore, that nineteenth-century theatregoers regarded the closet scene in *Hamlet* as the key to evaluating the quality of a production and the ability of the actor playing the title role. Indeed, the scene was often performed alone as a set piece.[45] Charles Lamb writes in 1802 that 'nine parts in ten of what Hamlet does, are transactions between himself and his moral sense, they are the effusions of his solitary musings, which he retires to holes and corners and the most sequestered parts of the palace to pour forth.' It is not surprising then that 'our curiosity is excited, when a new Hamlet or a new Richard makes his appearance, in the first place to inquire, how he acted in the Closet scene, in the Tent scene; how he looked, and how he started, when the Ghost came on.'[46] Of course, both of these scenes involve ghosts (one might even claim Richard's dream in the tent as proto-expressionist) which appear in private space and only to a single character (a description that also applies to the appearance of Caesar's ghost to Brutus). Yet Hamlet's closet scene is the more curious of the two because there is another person in the room at the time of his vision. Critics like Lamb were especially interested in the problem of representing the solipsized mind. In *Wilhelm Meister*, Goethe proposes to represent subjective vision by using a life-sized portrait of the King with the Ghost posing exactly like the figure in the portrait. Then, when the Ghost leaves the stage, Hamlet stares after the apparition and his mother at the picture, giving the impression that only Hamlet has actually seen the spectre. But, as Edwin Booth recognized, the scene is less concerned with representing Hamlet's vision than with representing the problem of interiority on stage. Booth's Hamlet becomes increasingly desperate when the Queen cannot see the spectre.

One of the many questions raised by the play is why the Ghost is visible to all the characters on stage in the first act, on the ramparts in the open air, but in the closet scene only to Hamlet.[47] The way to address this important inconsistency is to consider not only the different characters that are involved but also the different kinds of space. For if the walls of Elsinore serve as a metaphor for the parameters of the self, with Hamlet we have, following this architectural logic, moved deeper into the problem of subjectivity as we enter the play's most disquietingly private space. In space and dialogue, the scene presents a structural homology between ghost sighting and soul searching. Now Hamlet 'will set [Gertrude] up a glass / Where [she] may see the inmost part of [herself]' (3.4.20–1). Hamlet's obsession with the hidden, the invisible (e.g., 'the unseen good old man' [4.1.12]), is expressed here with particular emphasis upon the metaphor of body and soul; the Ghost instructs Hamlet to step between his mother and 'her fighting soul,' for 'Conceit in weakest bodies strongest works' (3.4.117–18). But Gertrude has already delved dangerously inward. Hamlet's badgering ('Have you eyes? ... Ha, have you eyes?') leads her to turn her 'eyes into

[her] very soul' (3.4.65–8, 3.4.89). No one in the theatre can verify what Hamlet has seen in the two miniatures of father and stepfather, and we can assume that Gertrude cannot either. Nor can we see the Queen's soul, though we take her word for it that she can. So, when Hamlet turns *his* eyes upon the theatrical representation of a ghost, why should the audience suspend disbelief and share his point of view instead of suspending disbelief and sharing that of his more empirical and, in this case, sympathetic mother?

> Alas, how is't with you,
> That you do bend your eye on vacancy,
> And with th' incorporal air do hold discourse? (3.4.116–18)

The Queen sees *nothing*, represented by an actor in the costume of Hamlet's father, 'Nothing at all, yet all that is I see.' Of course, the King (Hamlet's father? Claudius?) *is* 'a thing . . . of *nothing*' (4.2.29–31). In the closet scene, the Ghost's new selectivity about whom it appears to is, therefore, a consequence, not of the logic of the plot, but of space, insofar as space has thematic significance. If the King is a thing of nothing, *he* can only be seen, or, as Horatio might say, 'a piece of him' can, when appearing in specific spaces, such as the ramparts or the space of the stage itself. This architectural logic is investigated repeatedly in the modern drama through the trope of the haunted house, by drawing the attention of characters that in an opening scene are outside to thresholds and, often, moving them into the house itself as the play advances. The action of Strindberg's *Ghost Sonata* draws the eyes of the central characters from the initial action in a public square to the doors and windows of a fashionable house and ultimately into its deepest recesses. And the first words of Yeats's Old Man in *Purgatory* are 'Study that house.'

The early decades of the nineteenth century saw the development of a technology as both popular entertainment and widespread metaphor that, in effect, made Hamlets of everyone. In 1798, literally using smoke and mirrors or what was known as the 'magic-lantern,' the Belgian inventor and student of optics Étienne-Gaspard Robertson presented what he called the first 'fantasmagorie' in Paris. In her fascinating article 'Phantasmagoria: Spectral Technologies and the Metaphorics of Modern Reverie,' Terry Castle recounts Robertson's wonderful chicanery. The audience is locked in the 'Salle de la Fantasmagorie'; a candle is extinguished; muffled sounds of wind and thunder fill the claustrophobic space; unearthly music emanates from a glass harmonica; and

Robertson himself morbidly delivers a speech on death, immortality, and 'the unsettling power of superstition and fear to create terrifying illusions.' Then, one by one, mysterious luminous shapes began to surge and flicker over the heads of the spectators.[48]

As a showman of ghosts, Robertson soon made his fortune, despite a raft of imitators. Phantasmagoria shows quickly became a staple in London, for example, often dramatizing literary classics and pseudo-historical events, including Shakespeare's various ghosts, the raising of Samuel by the witch at Endor, the transformation of Louis XVI into a skeleton, and later Dickens's 'The Haunted Man.' Like the recently invented stereoscope, phantasmagoria shows were literally *obscene*. They 'shattered the *scenic* relationship between viewer and object that was intrinsic to the fundamentally theatrical setup of the camera obscura.'[49] At least, they contributed to a re-imagining of the theatrical. Though it may be hard to appreciate in the radically visual culture of the twenty-first century, contemporary audiences of phantasmagoria were often terrified at what they perceived as real ghosts coming at them.

Castle demonstrates not only the importance of phantasmagoria as popular entertainment around the turn of the century but also the pervasiveness of the terminology. Goethe's Werther, for instance, desperately in love with Lotte, speaks of seeing her inside his head: 'In this hovel, this solitary place ... your image, the memory of you, suddenly overwhelmed me ... I seem to be standing before a sort of raree show, watching the little men and little horses jerk before my eyes; and I often ask myself if everything is not an optical illusion.'[50] Castle argues that, 'from an initial connection with something external and public (an artificially produced "spectral" illusion), the word has now come to refer to something wholly internal or subjective: the phantasmic imagery of the mind.'[51] But, while Castle identifies a crucial shift in metaphors for perception, she also re-inscribes the division between internal and external, merely shifting emphasis to the former. In fact, the example from Goethe indicates a deconstruction or mediation of the binary opposition of inside/outside, imaginary/sensory. Werther's 'vision' registers the phantasmal image of Lotte and the 'whole world' on the same plane of reality. Later, in Dickens's *Great Expectations* (1860), Pip too is subject to phantasmic visions, and, after seeing a production of *Hamlet*, imagines himself to 'play Hamlet to Miss Havisham's Ghost.'[52] Nonetheless, it is evident that this shift in the usage of ghosts as metaphors indicates, as Castle claims, a 'significant transformation in human consciousness over the past two centuries ... Even as we have come to discount the spirit-world of our ancestors and to equate seeing ghosts and apparitions with having 'too much' imagination, we have come increasingly to believe, as if through a kind of epistemological recoil, in the spectral nature of our own thoughts – to figure imaginative activity itself, paradoxically, as a kind of ghost-seeing.'[53] Seeing ghosts thus involves a notion that is paradoxically antitheatrical, an experience that is mental and private, not publicly verifiable.

'What begins in the 1820s and 1830s,' writes Crary, 'is a repositioning of the observer, outside of the fixed relations of interior/exterior presupposed by the camera obscura and into an undemarcated terrain on which the distinction between internal sensation and external signs is irrevocably blurred.'[54] Coleridge, who sees himself in Hamlet, worries about the hyperactive imagination ('sicklied o'er with the pale cast of thought'), which is turned not to the concrete reality without but to the insubstantial one within, 'giving substance to shadows.' The 'glittering eye' of the ancient mariner, for instance, is not only turned upon the outer world but also an inner eye:

> I closed my lids, and kept them close,
> And the balls like pulses beat;
> For the sky and the sea, and the sea and the sky
> Lay like a load on my weary eye,
> And the dead were at my feet.   ('Rime of the Ancient Mariner,' 4: 248–52)

This inner eye, not simply Hamlet's 'mind's eye,' much less Oedipus's sightless orbs, but the eyeball itself, still seeing yet veiled from the world by its lid, becomes a crucial metaphor for playwrights of the modern stage. The distinction between the abstract or spiritual workings of the mind and the physical workings of the body is eroded.

'What is light?' asks August Strindberg in 'A Glance into Space.' 'Something outside me or within, subjective perceptions?' He goes on to note that he can create the physical sensation of looking upon the sun by pressing on his lidded eyes: 'What is light when darkness is not its opposite, which may be easily confirmed by going into a dark room and pressing upon one's eyeballs ... When it is dark and I press on my eyeballs, I see first a chaos of lights, stars or sparks, which are gradually condensed and gathered up into a brilliant disk.'[55] Strindberg's approach to the problem of vision is physical, but he also explains that light is a force, not itself an element or a thing. As such it must be invisible until activated inside the body. Light is no respecter of spatial boundaries or of the gap between subject and object. Yet this formulation does imply a subject *in* which experience is located. The recent discovery of X-rays (1895) and the new ability to put cameras inside the body, as a Viennese surgeon did in 1898 to expose a pulsating heart, indicate the revolution in the natural sciences that supplies a context for Strindberg's visualizing human interiors.[56]

Significantly, in discussing the nature of light, Strindberg slides smoothly into and out of considering the locus of the self: 'Where does the self begin and where does it end? Has the eye adapted itself to the sun? Or does the eye create the phenomenon called the sun?' Strindberg's play *The Ghost Sonata* concludes with the trope of the sun raising radical questions about the problem of appearance, equating the sun paradoxically with hiddenness and theatricality with an invisible, spiritual experience. (The song begins: 'I saw the sun / I seemed to see the Hidden One.' And then the room 'disappears.')[57] All these questions inform an important new antitheatrical tendency in the modern drama. The conclusion of *The Ghost Sonata* seems a direct allusion to another crucial instance of that tendency, the conclusion of Ibsen's *Ghosts* (1881).

A ground-breaking experiment in dramatic realism, *Ghosts* represents a deep meditation on the duality of spirit and form, and specifically a notion of form that is rigid and absolute as opposed to one characterized by what Oswald calls the 'joy of life.'[58] Ibsen recognizes that a modern audience will accept the figurability of ghosts in language alone, as a metaphor for memory that is mental and biological and entirely natural (not supernatural). There is no need for ghostly props and make-up, music, smoke and mirrors. However, the central problem for Ibsen is not the representation of microscopic viruses or genetic inclinations that characters transmit to each other but that of the spirit and its realization in a form that is free or self-conscious.

Mrs Alving is haunted less by the return of the dead than by dead ideas, as well as by the possibility of 'free thinking' that is opposed to an existence that seeks to conform to ideals. But her anxiety about the ghosts that she cannot escape leads her to extend the idea of ghosts radically. We are all ghosts, as she tells Pastor Manders: 'It's not only what we inherit from our fathers and mothers that keeps on returning in us. It's all kinds of old dead doctrines and opinions and beliefs, that sort of thing ... I just have to pick up a newspaper, and it's as if I could see the ghosts slipping between the lines. They must be haunting our whole country, ghosts everywhere ... And there we are, the lot of us, so miserably afraid of the light.'[59] This ghostliness is paradoxically a form of unconsciousness, conformity, a lack of freedom, and a sense of radical instability, a sense of liminality or boundlessness. The drama will develop this paradox into two kinds of ghostliness. One kind requires external light but lacks that of the interior. This epistemological framework is rigid and implies a firm subject–object opposition. The other kind of ghostliness privileges internal space and is organic. The drama of *Ghosts* eventuates in a figurative slipping between the lines, when literal and metaphorical visions collide on the rampart walls of Oswald's self.

*Ghosts* brilliantly defines a split between two different kinds of seeing and two different kinds of ghosts. Consequently, the play represents a radical revision of the phenomenology of the stage, as the audience is forced to question what it means to see a ghost. The play's most stunning moment of ghostly representation is the ultimate moment and climax, a scene that takes us back to the mother-son closet scene in *Hamlet*. At the end of *Ghosts* Oswald shrinks into himself. He is completely solipsized by his inherited disease, and, paradoxically, his final collapse, the representation of his inwardness or interiority, is the *coup de théâtre*.

> Mrs Alving (*bending over him*): . . . And look, Osvald, what a lovely day we'll have. Bright sunlight. Now you can really see your home. (*She goes to the table and puts out the lamp. Sunrise. The glaciers and peaks in the background shine in the brilliant light of the morning. With his back toward the distant view, Osvald sits motionless in the armchair.*)
> Osvald (*abruptly*): Mother, give me the sun.
> Mrs Alving (*by the table, looks at him startled*): What did you say?
> Osvald (*repeats in a dull monotone*): The sun. The sun.
> Mrs Alving (*moves over to him*): Osvald, what is the matter? (*Osvald seems to crumple inwardly in the chair; all his muscles loosen; the expression leaves his face; and his eyes stare blankly.*)
> Mrs Alving (*shaking with fear*): What is it? (*In a shriek.*) Osvald! What's wrong! (*Drops to her knees beside him and shakes him.*) Osvald! Osvald! Look at me! Don't you know me?
> Osvald (*in the same monotone*): The sun – the sun.
> Mrs Alving (*springs to her feet in anguish, tears at her hair with both hands, and screams*): I can't bear this! (*Whispers as if paralyzed by fright.*) I can't bear it! . . . No, no, no! – Yes! – No, no! (*She stands a few steps away from him, her fingers thrust into her hair, staring at him in speechless horror.*)
> Osvald (*sitting motionless, as before*): The sun – the sun.

Like *Hamlet, Ghosts* raises basic problems of theatrical representation. Oswald becomes most untheatrical, most inexpressive in this terrifying moment of collapse. He is unreadable (or uninterpretable). Notably, like Hamlet, Mrs Alving, the witness, is paralysed. The problem of what to do is activated by the epistemological problem: What is Oswald's status? What is the matter with him? What is going on, in this case, *inside* of him? She sees the ambiguous ghost, in effect, as her son's eyes are turned to his very soul – the sun, like self-knowledge, associated with Apollo through the long tradition of the Western stage. And *Ghosts* evokes important aspects of *Oedipus* in structure and theme.[60] Oswald's vision is an inner vision, and yet he is, unlike Oedipus, a ghost of himself, seeing himself seeing.[61]

For Peter Szondi, the interiority of Ibsen's characters is a fundamental formal problem; their truth is that of interiority: 'There lie the motives for the decisions that emerge in the light of day; there the traumatic effects of these decisions lie hidden and live on despite all external changes.' The dramas of Ibsen thus lack not only a temporal present but also a topical one. The modern drama, as Szondi defines it, originated in the Renaissance as an entirely self-enclosed form. It is absolute in the sense that it does not acknowledge (and implicitly does not require) an audience. The absolute drama represents the totality of life; it is interpersonal. But Ibsen's figures are solitary and estranged, turned inward. That means, for Szondi, that Ibsen cannot give his thematic 'direct dramatic presentation. This material has need of the analytical technique, and not simply to achieve greater density ... The thematic ultimately remains alien to the stage. However much the thematic is tied to the presence ... of an action, it remains exiled in the past and the depths of the individual.'[62]

But Szondi's theory is insufficiently developed on at least two levels: the notion of the absolute, modern (Renaissance) drama is not based upon concrete examples from theatre history or dramatic texts. Presumably any careful exegesis of particular Renaissance dramas would reveal challenges to the straightforwardly 'mimetic' model. We have already seen ways in which Shakespeare's theatre, and *Hamlet* in particular, may subvert Szondi's theory of the drama's origins. Szondi's notion of the objective is limited by his persistent, underlying assumption that the drama is mimetic – holding the mirror up to nature. 'The Drama of modernity,' he writes, 'was the result of a newly self-conscious being [Renaissance man] who, after the collapse of the medieval worldview, sought to create an artistic reality within which he could *fix and mirror himself* on the basis of interpersonal relationships alone.'[63] But this notion is inadequately historicized, and the notion of the absolute Drama is too rigid, relying on a stable (and absolute) notion of objectivity. Szondi's fiction–reality dichotomy does not allow for the crucial space *in-between*, the space of performance and of ghosts. Ghosts, by definition, transgress boundaries, of present–past, material–spiritual, real–imaginary.

Instead of adhering to or rejecting a monolithic concept of form, nineteenth-century dramatists sought a notion of form that is organic (a metaphor exemplified by Oswald's condition). The idea of organicism, articulated in Coleridge's lectures, in contrast to 'mechanical' form, implies a more fluid process of mediation and self-consciousness. Later, Henri Bergson would define drama in a way that erases the line between internal and external and seeks to reconcile the subjective and the objective: 'A drama, even when portraying passions or vices that bear a name, so completely incorporates them in the person that their names are forgotten, their general characteristics effaced, and we no longer think of them at all, but rather of the person *in whom they are assimilated.*'[64]

The organic form of drama is most clearly suggested in Bergson's use of the word 'gracefulness' [*la grâce*]. Gracefulness is not imposed from without but generated from within. Gracefulness is 'the immateriality which ... passes into matter.'[65] In this formulation, the soul, or what Bergson elsewhere calls the *élan vital*, the life force, shapes the matter that contains it. The soul is not immobilized by matter, as it is in comedy, but remains infinitely supple and perpetually in motion. In drama, we forget the soul's materiality and think only of its vitality. Thus, Bergson concludes, in every *human form*, our imagination 'sees the effort of a soul which is shaping matter, a soul which is infinitely supple and perpetually in motion.' Drama, according to this vision, represents the immateriality that passes into matter, the *inner* life of the soul.

The Proteus chapter of James Joyce's *Ulysses* represents this 'modern' understanding of the drama and of *Hamlet* in particular. There, the melancholy Stephen Dedalus, in his 'Hamlet hat,' is deeply unsettled because he has not been able adequately to give form to the ghosts that haunt him and, since they are internal, he remains deeply self-alienated: 'My soul walks with me, form of forms. So in the moon's midwatches I pace the path above the rocks, in sable silvered, hearing Elsinore's tempting flood.'[66] In a vision of haunting beauty, Joyce conflates Hamlet, Hamlet's father (of the 'sable silvered' beard), and Stephen, the ghost and the hero's own soul.[67] But he also tellingly articulates the central problem of Shakespeare's play: the formal realization of the formless soul.

Szondi had argued that by trying to reveal the hidden life of his characters, Ibsen killed them. But, of course, Ibsen does not kill Oswald, who is still alive at the end of the play. Szondi's analysis instead reveals the creativity of the spectator who is drawn so often by Ibsen to transgress the limits of his dramas, to project his imagination between the lines or outside of the structural limits of the plays altogether. Spectators have been unable to resist speculating about what happens to Nora after she makes her final exit, crossing the visible boundaries of the stage and the temporal boundaries of the play, just as her first action had been to enter the space of visibility. A Doll's House may be especially susceptible to creative interpretations precisely because the spatial boundaries of the play are so insistently thematized.[68] But Joyce comically reveals where the impulse of the spectator may lead when applied to Ghosts. In 'Epilogue to Ibsen's "Ghosts,"' Joyce imagines the return of the ghost of Captain Alving as a speaking part:

Dear quick, whose conscience buried deep
The grim old grouser [Ibsen himself] has been salving
Permit one spectre more to peep.
I am the ghost of Captain Alving.[69]

Like the ghost of Hamlet's father, the ghost of Captain Alving returns to expose some dirty doings, namely, that Oswald may not be his son after all but Pastor Manders's. But Joyce, whose novels represent, like Ibsen's dramas, the notion that children are the ghosts of their parents, plays as usual with multiple levels of irony. And this poem, written in the first person, indirectly acknowledges an artistic paternity that breaks down the boundaries of authorship. Joyce is the ghost of Ibsen, just as every spectator can, in some sense, be an author of the play. After all, as Mrs Alving says, we are all ghosts.

The expressivist reaction against the boundaries imposed by modern society connects playwrights as diverse as Ibsen and Oscar Wilde. Wilde remarks through a character, Vivian, in 'The Decay of Lying' that the 'unfortunate aphorism about Art holding the mirror up to Nature is deliberately said by Hamlet in order to convince the bystanders of his absolute insanity in all art matters.'[70] For Wilde, Life imitates Art, which is not to say simply that external or material beauty is produced by a more real inner or spiritual one, but that the imagination constitutes reality for the eye. Nature herself is our creation: 'It is in our brain that she quickens to life. Things are because we see them, and what we see, and how we see it, depends on the Arts that have influenced us. To look at a thing is very different from seeing a thing. One does not see anything until one sees its beauty. Then, and then only, does it come into existence.'[71] The 'wonderful brown fogs that come creeping down our streets' we get from the Impressionists. Although Wilde served a long intellectual apprenticeship in the fine arts, under Ruskin and Pater at Oxford and Whistler in London, he would ultimately privilege literature as chief among the arts, subordinating the vision of the eye to that of the mind's eye. 'The image stained upon the canvas possesses no spiritual element of growth or change,' Wilde writes in 'The Critic as Artist.' 'Movement, that problem of the visible arts, can be truly realised by Literature alone.'[72] Nowhere is this problem of the visual arts clearer than in *The Picture of Dorian Gray*; a painter is murdered, but in the narrative a painting comes alive.

Wilde's work and life are pervaded by his continual deconstruction of the binary opposition between body and soul or matter and spirit, as well as that of subject and object, seer and seen. As Basil Hallward says in the novella, 'Every portrait that is painted with feeling is a portrait of the artist.'[73] And that remark about perception is deeply related to Lord Henry's comment to Dorian that 'nothing can cure the soul but the senses, just as nothing can cure the senses but the soul.' In *Dorian Gray* Wilde so deeply integrates literature and painting that he creates what may be described as his most theatrical work. Disaster befalls the actress Sibyl Vane ('the wonderful soul that is hidden away in that little ivory body'), but that is because in the end she gave up art for reality. 'Dorian, Dorian,' she exclaims, 'before I knew you, acting was the one reality of my life. It was only in the theatre that I lived ... I believed in everything ... The painted scenes were my world. I knew nothing but shadows, and I thought them real. You came – oh, my beautiful love! – and you freed my soul from prison. You taught me what reality really is.' But the shadows were real. In Wilde's world, to be is to embrace *seems*. 'The Fisherman and His Soul,' one of Wilde's extraordinarily lyrical fairy tales represents a similar meditation on freedom and form; in it a young man literally cuts away his Soul ('not the shadow of the body, but ... the body of the Soul')[74] for love of a little mermaid. He achieves a higher wholeness only when, with the death of his beloved, his Soul re-enters his body through his broken heart. The life of the soul requires the form of the body imagined through art in order to express itself: 'I shall show you my soul,' Dorian tells Hallward. 'You shall see the thing that you fancy only God can see.'[75]

'Aesthetics are higher than ethics,' Wilde writes in 'The Critic as Artist'; 'they belong to a more spiritual sphere.' Wilde's artistic vision vividly represents the dangers (and often the comedy) of rigid conceptions of form, subject–object polarities, and the reifying gaze. 'The Fisherman and His Soul,' for example, explicitly echoes the language of Wilde's most sustained meditation on vision in dramatic form: *Salomé*. As that play begins, like *Hamlet*, on the margins of the palace, the soldiers are spectators commenting on the act of seeing:

> *First Soldier*: The Tetrarch has a sombre look.
> *Second Soldier*: Yes; he has a sombre look.
> *First Soldier*: He is looking at something.
> *Second Soldier*: He is looking at someone.
> . . .
> *First Soldier*: The Jews worship a God that you cannot see.
> *The Cappadocian*: I cannot understand that.
> *First Soldier*: In fact, they only believe in things that you cannot see.
> *The Cappadocian*: That seems to me altogether ridiculous.[76]

The presence of Jews in Herod's court enables direct consideration of the quasi-theological problem of theatrical representation, since the prohibition against representing God in any image is a central feature of Judaic theology (the second of the Ten Commandments). Herod, the potently gazing Tetrarch, is afraid of Jokanaan because 'he is a man who has seen God'; he has performed a simultaneously transcendent and subversive act of vision. 'That cannot be,' replies a Jew, expressing what the play will show to be ultimately an even more effectively subversive notion. 'There is no man who hath seen God since the prophet Elias. He is the last man who saw God. In these days God doth not show himself. He *hideth* himself.'[77] This statement is challenged and made more radical by Another Jew: 'Verily, no man knoweth if Elias the prophet did indeed see God. Peradventure it was but the shadow of God that he saw.' The debate is extended through a Fifth Jew who insists: 'No one can tell how God worketh ... There is *no knowledge of any thing*.' Wilde, the most self-conscious of playwrights, predicates the suspension of disbelief in both theatre and religion on the impossibility of certainty.

'The very essence of romance is uncertainty,' remarks Algernon in *The Importance of Being Earnest*, reflecting ironically not just on romance but also on Romanticism: that is, on the Romantic model of philosophical thought expressed through sensuous means, or as embodied meaning, that characterized Hegel and Coleridge. This twist on the idioms of 'essence' and 'uncertainty' indicates both an extension of the Romantic challenge to the Enlightenment utopia of aesthetic transparency and, by the late nineteenth century, an increasing sense of the limitations of Romantic epistemology and nostalgia for a supposedly more authentic or immediate way of seeing things.

God's province is absolute, as Elaine Scarry comments, 'precisely because he is unlimited by any specifying acts of representation.'[78] Scarry's discussion of scriptural wounding and physical pain indicates the value of John the Baptist as a site of representation in Wilde's play and in the theatre generally. If an object of belief, such as God, cannot be represented, the body of the believer must serve as evidence of that belief, in effect, turning belief inside-out. The theatrical context in which the wounded body is to be displayed, the altar for example, 'externalizes and makes visible the shape of belief.' Jokanaan repeatedly resists visual representation; for much of the play he is present on stage only as a disembodied voice. Ultimately, in *Salomé* the silver platter that frames the severed head serves a paradoxical function, for Jokanaan's resistance both has and has not been effective.

Like 'The Fisherman and His Soul,' this relentlessly visual drama associates the lust of the eyes with death. Significantly, both Jokanaan (in a cistern) and the little mermaid (in the sea) resist entering a space where they can be seen. 'Who is this woman who is looking at me?' asks Jokanaan when he is brought forth by force. 'I will not have her look at me. Wherefore does she look at me with her golden eyes, under her gilded eyelids? I know not who she is. I do not wish to know who she is.' The 'lust of the eyes' (ascribed to virtually all the characters in the play but Jokanaan) seems to presuppose what Kant calls 'accessory' or 'dependent' beauty (*pulchritudo adhaerens*). In Kant's view, beauty 'concerns only form,' so if it is connected with 'the agreeable (the sensation),' as in the beauty (desirability) of a human being, the purity of a judgment of taste is impaired. 'If a judgment about beauty is mingled with the least interest,' writes Kant, 'then it is partial and not a pure judgment of taste. In order to play the judge in matters of taste, we must not be in the least biased in favor of the thing's existence but must be wholly indifferent about it.'[79] Herod's lust for Salomé's body leads him to a crisis of the spirit ('What she has done is a great crime. I am sure that it was a crime against an unknown God.'), culminating in an execution of invisibility: Salomé is crushed beneath soldiers' shields instead of being decapitated herself as Wilde first planned. Wilde demonstrates dramatically (actively) and theatrically (visually) that Kant's transcendental idealism cannot form the basis of a modern way of seeing things, for Wilde's mode of imagining of aesthetic beauty is, for all his disclaimers, resolutely social and shaped by desire.

Despite his reputation as an aesthete, Wilde appeals not to a notion of aesthetic purity but to a profound notion of freedom in the Hegelian, as opposed to the Kantian, sense. Once Jokanaan emerges he is fixed by the reifying gaze; like the little mermaid and Sybil Vane, he has a body as white as ivory. Yet, as Wilde writes in 'The Soul of Man under Socialism,' 'Despotism is unjust to everybody, including the despot ...; all authority is quite degrading.'[80] Those who watch and those who are watched are equally imprisoned in *Salomé* because all are equally isolated or lacking in consciousness. The lusts of the body result in 'a crime against an unknown God.' And Salomé herself crosses a horrifying boundary or threshold as she plants her living lips upon the dead mouth of Jokanaan. Herod, of course, is trapped by his word to commit a deed that will condemn him for the rest of history. 'It is true, I have looked at you all this evening,' he says to Salomé. 'Your beauty troubled me. Your beauty has grievously troubled me, and I have looked at you too much. But I will look at you no more. Neither at things, nor at people should one look. Only in mirrors should one look, for mirrors do but show us masks.' The lust of the eyes precludes self-consciousness. Indeed, so resistant to consciousness is Herod that the drama's climax makes of him an inverted Claudius. At least Claudius is self-conscious. As Herod rises from watching the play-within-the-play (Salomé's dance), he reverses Claudius's call for light, crying, 'Put out the torches. I will not look at things, I will not suffer things to look at me. Put out the torches!'[81]

Like Hamlet, Salomé is both the observed of all observers and a deadly spectator herself. And, like Hamlet, she is a self-conscious performer whose stepfather/spectator has incestuously married her mother. Salomé's gender, therefore, is both less and more important than most previous critics have recognized. The play does represent an exploitative, masculine gaze through the character of Herod, but the audience can experience a more sophisticated kind of seeing, especially if Wilde's doctrine of the 'truth of masks' is realized in production. Although the play has invited both misogynist and feminist readings, as John Paul

Riquelme compellingly shows, in writing the part for the middle-aged Sarah Bernhardt, Wilde 'affects our conceptions of the role and of the audience's likely response':

> The refraction of the audience's vision caused by a mature dancer affects the issue of Herod's relation and our own to the dance ... In Bernhardt's casting as Salomé, we experience an obvious form of doubling through the contradictory linking of young and old, in which the actress becomes during the performance something that she obviously is not. Through an unveiling that the actress's doubling makes possible the audience has the chance to recognize itself as different from its conventional view of itself.[82]

According to this reading, Salomé occupies a borderline space in terms of both gender and conventional ways of looking. Riquelme also notes that Bernhardt in the 1890s was famous for playing male roles and, especially, for playing Hamlet. Bernhardt herself explained her attraction to the 'subtle' and 'torturous' character of Hamlet, by remarking, 'It is not male parts, but male brains that I prefer.'[83]

Herod's conception of the mirror as a reflector of things outside the self, superficial images or masks, indicates an inadequate conception of the relation between mind and reality; in this sense, his remark is not unlike Hamlet's relatively pedestrian instructions to the players. The significance of Wilde's paradoxical revision of the metaphor becomes evident in 'The Fisherman,' in which the Soul, travelling independently, is shown the Mirror of Wisdom:

> It reflecteth all things that are in heaven and on earth, save only the face of him who looketh into it. This it reflecteth not, so that he who looketh into it may be wise. Many other mirrors are there, but they are mirrors of Opinion. This only is the Mirror of Wisdom. And they who possess this mirror know everything, nor is there anything hidden from them.[84]

The central paradox in this passage is in the word 'reflect,' for properly speaking the Mirror of Wisdom does not reflect; it is an emblem for *knowing* through the interplay between self and other, not the ordinary chiasmic relation of self to itself in a mirror. And the first sentence echoes Hamlet's own wiser words to Horatio, 'There are more things in heaven and earth ... / Than are dreamt of in your philosophy' (1.5.168–9).

In his influential work *The Mirror and the Lamp*, M.H. Abrams describes a paradigm shift around 1800 (or the publication of Wordsworth's preface to *Lyrical Ballads*) in the history of literary criticism. Abrams's title identifies two common and antithetic metaphors of mind: the first typifying much thinking from Plato to the eighteenth century, the second indicative of Romantic conceptions of creativity. Rejecting a 'mimetic' model, he argues that 'romantic predications about poetry, or about art in general, turn on a metaphor [the lamp] which, like "overflow," signifies the internal made external. The most frequent of these terms was "expression."'[85] Wilde articulates this notion explicitly in 'The Critic as Artist.' 'The highest criticism,' he writes, 'is the record of one's own soul.'[86]

The mind invests the sensuous world with spiritual reality, and form, far from obtaining any absolute existence apart from the mind, is, as Hegel writes, 'born – born again, that is – of the mind.'[87] The Romantic notion that the soul could be perpetually reborn, Richard Ellmann writes, was one that Wilde particularly liked.[88] For Hegel, beauty is fundamentally self-conscious, characterized by 'intellectual being and by freedom.'[89] The natural world, by contrast, is only a reflection of the beauty that resides in the mind: 'In its own being, a natural existence such as the sun is indifferent, is not free or self-conscious.'

In a 1909 tribute to his fallen countryman, suggestively titled 'Oscar Wilde: The Poet of "Salomé,"' James Joyce considers Wilde's deathbed conversion to Catholicism, the act of spiritual dedication with which he closed the spiritual rebellion of his life:

> In his last book, *De Profundis*, he kneels before a gnostic Christ . . . and then his true soul, trembling, timid, and saddened, shines through the mantle of Heliogabalus. His fantastic legend, his opera [*Salomé*] – a polyphonic variation on the rapport of art and nature, but at the same time a revelation of his own psyche – his brilliant books sparkling with epigrams . . . these are now divided booty.[90]

The metaphor of division operates on multiple levels, for the division of Wilde's legacy is viewed in relation to the rapport of art and nature in his play, on the one hand, and the truth of his own soul that shone through the profligacy of his body, on the other. For Joyce notions of wholeness and fragmentation, mediated and complicated in his own later work by the transmigration of souls, are pervasive concerns. And nowhere is Wilde more poignantly invoked by Joyce than in the Proteus chapter of *Ulysses*, with just an allusion to Wilde's *Requiescat*, the poem he wrote about his dead sister Isola. 'Tread lightly, she is near' it begins.

Stephen Dedalus, meanwhile, is surrounded by his own ghosts (not all of the them of the dead), not to mention the vexing 'imp hypostasis.'

The spirit becomes self-aware in recognizing self in other, a continual play of antithetical forces. Hegel's phenomenology extends logically into aesthetics, for the 'beauty of art is the beauty that is born ... of the mind [*geist*],' for the mind or spirit alone is capable of truth. This challenge of the very distinction between inner and outer realms again constitutes a radical departure from the eighteenth-century thinkers Eliot had praised. Hegel writes:

> Now, this whole sphere of the empirical and outer world is just what is not the world of genuine reality, but is to be entitled a mere appearance more strictly than is true of art ... Genuine reality is only to be found beyond the immediacy of feeling and of external object. Nothing is genuinely real but that which is ... the substance of nature and of mind ... Art liberates the real import of appearances from the semblance and deception of this bad and fleeting world, and imparts to phenomenal semblances a higher reality, born of mind.[91]

The inner is not substituted for or privileged over the outer. For Hegel the 'mind's eye' is not an inner, hallucinatory site but a metaphor for the experience of the spirit through sensuous form; later this incarnation of the mind's eye is realized in Emerson's metaphor for the poet himself as a transparent eyeball, an idea that is both physical and mystical. The binary opposition between inner and outer breaks down. Thus, 'real works of art are those where content and form exhibit a thorough identity.'[92]

The union between form and content in art, or between the human individual and nature in spirit, is, in short, deeply related to theories of subjective vision. Goethe had written that, 'in directing our attention to ... physical colours, we find it quite possible to place an objective phenomenon beside a subjective one, and often by means of the union of the two successfully penetrate farther into the nature of appearance.'[93] This protest against the Enlightenment view of phenomena, including human beings, as subjects and objects of objective, scientific analysis, insists on the creative role of the spectator or viewer in the act of seeing. '"To see the object as in itself it really is,"' writes Wilde's teacher Walter Pater, 'has been justly said to be the aim of all true criticism whatever; and in aesthetic criticism the first step towards seeing one's object as it really is, is to know one's own impression as it really is, to discriminate it, to realize it distinctly.'[94] Continuous with Pater's explicitly Hegelian theory of art, Werner Heisenberg's uncertainty principle, published in 1927 ('On the Perceptual Content of Quantum Theoretical Kinematics and Mechanics') showed that it is impossible for anyone to know at any instant the velocity and position of an electron, a problem of knowing that is fundamentally a problem of seeing. For if an observer shines enough light on an electron to see it, the light itself will change the electron's velocity. The material world, assuming that it exists, is ultimately not 'seeable' (*anschaulisch*).

If the poetic mind is a lamp, as Abrams suggests of both the Romantics and the moderns, then the world they illuminate is altered in the very process of perception. Consequently, in a perverse twist of the Romantic epistemology, the mind is potentially always unsure, always isolated and alone. 'The eye's plain version is a thing apart,' writes Wallace Stevens.[95] For the theatre, the problem of invisibility, then, provokes the further problem of the possibility of communal experience or even of any social experience. Plays, like ghosts, vanish when the lights come on. Claudius's cry – 'Give me some light!' (*Hamlet*, 3.2.269) – dissolves the play-within-the-play just as the dawn dissolves the spectre, or as the physicist alters the course of the electron. On the rising of the sun, ghosts depart to the borne from which no travellers return; yet, on future nights, as ghosts, they come again.

# 3 Samuel Beckett's *spectres du noir*: The Being of Painting and the Flatness of *Film*

*Listen. Before I go I will tell you this. I am your soul and all your souls. When I am gone you are dead . . . When I leave you I take with me all that has made you what you are – I take your significance and importance and all the accumulations of human instinct and appetite and wisdom and dignity. You will be left with nothing behind you and nothing to give to the waiting ones. Woe to you when they find you out! Good-bye!*

Although I thought this speech was rather far-fetched and ridiculous, he was gone and I was dead.

Flann O'Brien, *The Third Policeman*

I waited for my image to come back, I watched it as it trembled towards an ever increasing likeness. Now and then a drop, falling from my face, shattered it again. I did not see a soul all day.

Samuel Beckett, *Molloy*

In charting a history of 'seeing things' in modernity, I have focused in the central chapters of this book on two crucial nodal points, the first being the coalescence of diverse readings of *Hamlet* around the problem of visualizing human interiority and representing that vision in theatrical terms. *Hamlet* becomes the key text through which Romantic and post-Romantic audiences explored and enacted newly fluid and theatrical models of subjectivity. In the present chapter, I turn to Samuel Beckett's *Film*, his art criticism, and many of his other works, to question modernism's collapse of the self into the materiality of expressive media, a fall of the subject, in Beckett's devastatingly sceptical vision, into thing-ness. Without attempting a full-fledged definition of modernism, this chapter employs the term to indicate historical and philosophical developments in the twentieth century still under the rubric of modernity: the extension of inwardness in art (e.g., from the 'expressivist' to the 'expressionist') along with the decentring of the subject. It further assumes, in spite of modernist artists' rebellion against aspects of Romantic spiritualism and greater emphasis on the media or language of art, modernism's reliance, in general, on a Romantic prototype of spiritual reality *within*.

From the 'stupid obsession with depth' of *The Unnamable* to 'flatness endless' of *Lessness*, Beckett rejects the speculative theory of human interiority that characterizes the work of key modernist authors, dramatists, artists, and critics. I situate Beckett's exploration of flatness in several contexts: Romantic theories of perception and a related pictorial dramaturgy, the twentieth-century phenomenological tradition and post-war art criticism, media relationships Beckett chose as sites of investigation (written text, painting, theatre, film, and television), and Protestant iconoclasm. In describing both physical and metaphysical flatness, I develop the relationship identified in this chapter's title between flatness and *spectres*. The latter are introduced in Beckett's art criticism, but his work is pervaded by the words *spirit, soul,* and *ghost*. Flatness and ghosts, the two central tropes of this chapter, are crucial not only metaphorically but also formally in painting and other arts that make use of surfaces. That is why the medium of film and Beckett's art criticism are central. In *Film* Beckett literalizes flatness.

Film clearly bears important relationships both to dramatic enactment in theatre and to the pictorial realism of photography. In achieving a partial synthesis of the two forms, film also extends fundamental debates about representation that are endemic to each. The metaphysics of human interiority is one of the oldest and most vital concerns shared by theatre and the visual arts. Consider a classic moment in Buster Keaton's *Steamboat Bill, Jr.* Buster, standing before a mirror in a hat store, seems to stare at his reflection while various hats are placed upon his head, spoofing the theatrical notion that character inheres in costume or, as Hamlet would have it, in trappings. But the image is also a subtle variation on the 'mirror held up to nature,' for the camera and, ultimately, the audience members have taken the place of the mirror. Describing this famous scene, Gilberto Perez detects in the image on screen a 'quality of introspective monologue, an apprehensive meditation on [the character's] own condition.' Because the audience imagines Buster to be looking at his own image, not out at them, the effect is of looking *into* him. 'It is Keaton's genius as an actor,' Perez writes, to keep a face so nearly deadpan and yet render it, by subtle inflections, so vividly expressive of inner life. His large deep eyes are the most eloquent feature; with merely a stare he can convey a wide range of emotions, from longing to mistrust, from puzzlement to sorrow ... At the haberdashery, without the trappings of a Boston collegian, he stares into the mirror and sees for the first time the hopeless discrepancy between his inner being and any of the roles he may have to assume in his dealings with the external world.[1]

The movie screen itself, however, being more like a canvas than a stage, can offer only the illusion of depth or inwardness.[2] The screen itself is literally flat.

In *Film,* Beckett pushes the figurative and literal flatness of the image to a *breaking* point. The tearing of a print, the 'destruction of God's image,' is followed by an even more radical iconoclasm, the tearing of photographs of people, an anti-poetics or unmaking not only of the theophanic but also ultimately of the autophanic image.[3] In exposing the vulnerability of the pictorial surface, destroying the support upon which an image appears, Beckett's figures radically critique the modernist paradox of flatness as a *desideratum,* a positive limitation, constitutive even of the negative. O's tearing of photographs is anticipated in *Malone Dies:* 'In the end Macmann tore up this photograph [of his lover Moll] and threw the bits in the air, one windy day. Then they scattered, though all subjected to the same conditions, as though with alacrity.'[4] The 'conditions' are uniformly physical, the paper animated by wind not spirit.

*Film,* in its combination of text (philosophical slogans, drawing, directions), light, and celluloid, is a work that cannot be reduced to the movie alone, and so also raises questions about relationships between the flatness of the projected image and the flatness of the page. Elaine Scarry comments that in the verbal arts images 'acquire the vivacity of perceptual objects,' though unlike painting, music, sculpture, theatre, and film, they 'are almost wholly devoid of *actual* sensory content ... That imaginary vivacity comes about by reproducing the deep structure of perception.'[5] It is precisely the deep structure of perception that Beckett persistently questions in a wide range of writings. In *Film,* as in 'A Piece of Monologue,' another text that figures the tearing of photographic images, Beckett rejects the sustaining assumptions of a still prevalent Protestant poetics: Discourse does *not* give way to vision. What the text discloses can be described, at best, in two dimensions, like the page itself, as 'Dark shapeless blot on surface elsewhere white.'[6] In the face of a blank universe, in which one can know 'nothing more than a surface,' Molloy remarks, 'you would do better, at least no worse, to obliterate texts than to blacken margins, to fill in the holes of words till all is blank and flat.'[7]

In literalizing flatness, explicitly reacting against a speculative metaphysics and sacralization of art, Beckett questions the very being of art. The importance of painting and the capacity of surfaces (of mirrors, walls, the human body) to signify had been the subject of Beckett's earliest critical essays and fiction. This chapter will establish both the richness and the specificity of Beckett's manipulation of the trope of surfaces and of the analogy between painting and theatre in his work. That analogy has been a crucial component of dramatic theory since the Greeks, though it is in the eighteenth century, in the critical writings of Diderot, that a modern pictorial dramaturgy and related problems of *absorption* and *theatricality* are first and most influentially articulated.[8] Formal similarities between painting and theatre, especially in the iconography of character and the representation of interior experience, continue to inform the critical discourse that Beckett adopts and to which he offers a persistently radical and self-conscious revision. The 'stupid obsession with depth' of the nameless narrator in *The Unnamable* suggests not only an obsession but also the ambivalence at play from Beckett's earliest writing to the latest. 'I conceived *Molloy* and what followed,' Beckett is reported to have said, 'the day I realized my own stupidity.'[9] In nearly every work, he draws our attention to the media of art, the surface of paintings, the frame of the stage, the flatness of film, the television box, and language itself, yet his characters also seem continually tormented by the possibility of pure apperception. The human figures that appear in these media paradoxically present themselves and resist representation. They persistently *seem* to claim that truth is that of interiority, but then withdraw the claim as unverifiable: 'Ping elsewhere always there but that not known.'[10] In Beckett ontological problems are always agonizingly epistemological.

The problem of exteriorizing or making visible discreet and cognizable aspects of human experience has, to put it mildly, a vexed position in modern drama. The image of an actor with his back turned to the audience, privileged in the 1880s by André Antoine and August Strindberg and achieving iconic status later in the film performances of Marlon Brando, may stand as a symbol of protest against previous theatrical conventions. For many the persistent enactment of self-absorption is a sign of the drama's decline. Peter Szondi laments that for Ibsen 'truth is that of interiority.'[11] Characters who lack a core self, an inner truth, like the extraordinarily theatrical Peer Gynt, are *doomed*. On the other hand, at the stunning climax of *Ghosts* the diseased Oswald harps on a sun that he alone can see, an ironic reference, one assumes, to Oedipus humbled before the god of appearances. 'La beauté intérieure' and 'la vie profonde,' advocated by Maurice Maeterlinck, are represented, if at all, through silence and stillness. 'Il m'est arrivé de croire,' writes Maeterlinck, 'qu'un viellard assis dans son fauteuil, attendent simplement sous la lampe ... vivait en réalité d'une vie plus profonde, plus humaine et plus générale que l'amant qui étrangle sa maîtresse, le capitaine qui ramporse une victoire ou "l'époux qui venge son honneur."' (I have come to believe ... that an old man, seated in an armchair, waiting simply beneath his lamp ... lives in reality a deeper, more human and more universal life than the lover who strangles his mistress, the captain who conquers in battle, or 'the husband who avenges his honour.')[12]

As I showed in the previous chapter, a widespread re-imagining of the dramatic significance of interiority in the early decades of the nineteenth century is fundamental to what we think of today as the 'modern' drama. Hamlet becomes more radically introspective, and this development is deeply related to Hegel's view that 'genuine reality' is to be found not in the external or empirical world of appearance but in 'the substance of nature and mind.'[13] The metaphor of mind as lamp, an essentialist, quasi-theological and speculative (that is, anti-empirical or intuitive) metaphysics, in which the subject literally *informs* the external world, is, as many have shown before, a crucial aspect of Romantic thought.[14] And that subject–object dialectic pervades the works of key modernist and proto-modernist writers, as well as many of their most important critics.

The popular theatre continues to structure itself upon assumptions of inner life and expression; aspects of the internal are made external, synthesizing images, thoughts, and feelings. The working title of Arthur Miller's ghostly play *Death of a Salesman*, for example, was 'The Inside of His Head.' Yet *deeply* related to expressive theory is a corresponding assumption that the essence or core of the self passes show. As Martin Meisel remarks, 'Only recently in the Western tradition have we accepted the convention that true feeling is always inarticulate and ultimately inexpressible.'[15] That ghostliness of the inner self has been, therefore, the principal subject of countless theoretical and practical discussions of theatre. 'I . . . am well aware of the fact that everyone has his own interior life which he would like to bring out into the open,' says the *capocomico*, or director, in Pirandello's *Six Characters in Search of an Author.* 'But the difficulty is precisely this: to bring out into the open only what is important in reference to others; and at the same time to reveal through that little bit all of that unrevealed interior life!'[16] The director's mechanistic approach to performance is based upon the same ontological, if not practical, assumptions as Stanislavski's still highly influential theory that acting must reach a 'spiritual' or 'inner' life. The common quality shared by great actors, he writes, is that 'their bodies were at the call and beck of the inner demands of their wills.' 'The bond between body and soul is indivisible.' Fantasy, Stanislavski writes, calls up 'from its secret depths, beyond reach of consciousness, elements of already experienced emotions, and regroups them to correspond with the images which arise within us.'[17]

Stanislavski, like Arthur Miller, reflects an aesthetic that permits spectators to experience action from the inside, as it were, to empathize. And Pirandello, too, preoccupied though he is with the ambiguity of reality and fiction, assumes nonetheless the importance of the concepts of interior and exterior. Their structural relationship is central to his art. The climax of his greatest play, *Henry IV*, occurs when 'real' characters, posing as portraits, step forth from the frames where the canvases have been cut away and terrify the watching Henry. The action suggests that the illusion inside the picture frames was of flatness not of depth, but Pirandello has inverted the spectator's assumptions, not obviated them. Interiority remains a crucial determinant; the play concludes, like *Ghosts*, with characters desperate to fathom the image (Henry) at their centre.

In 1868, Alexandre Dumas fils had written in his preface to *Un père prodigue*, 'C'est une science d'optique et de perspective qui permet de dessiner un personnage, un caractère, une passion, une action de l'âme d'un seul trait de plume.' (It is the science of optics and of perspective which allows [the playwright] to depict a human being, a character, a passion, an action of the soul with just the stroke of the pen.)[18] In Dumas's view, the successful playwright must be a manipulator of the 'purely external actions of human beings,' making frescoes to be seen from a distance and lit from below. Yet the greatest playwright will combine this technical, superficial gift with the ability to write 'avec son coeur et son âme pour l'âme et pour le coeur de l'humanité' (with his heart and soul for the soul and the heart of humanity). The successful play, like a successful fresco, will be infused with a soul that is consumed by its beholders, and it is precisely the complicity between the work and the audience, in this view, that constitutes theatre.[19]

The idea that material flatness is the essential feature of pictorial art and that audience is the essential feature of theatre recurs frequently among modern theorists. It is central to the theory of the great French drama critic Francisque Sarcey in his 1876 *Essai d'une esthétique de théâtre:*

> Dans la peinture, il s'agit de représenter sur une surface plane des objets qui ont tous leurs côtés, et des scenes de la vie humaine, qui, dans la réalité, ont exigé pour se mouvoir un vaste espace profondeur ... Regardons de même pour l'art dramatique, s'il n'y a pas un fait aussi certain que peut l'être celui-là dans la peinture et qui soit également pour lui une condition absolue d'existence et de développement ... Il y a, quand on parle de théâtre, un fait qui ne saurait maquer de frapper les yeux les moins attentifs: c'est la présence d'un public.
>
> [Painting is about representing, on a plane surface, objects which have all their dimensions, and scenes from life, which, in reality, would require for their existence a vast depth of background ... In the same way let us inquire concerning dramatic art if there is not also a fact which corresponds to this fact in painting and which is in like manner the indispensable condition of its existence and development ... There is, in speaking of theatre, one fact that cannot fail to strike the eyes of the least attentive; it is the presence of a public.][20]

Sarcey's analogy is especially important for being so patently imperfect, since the 'means of expression' of painting is in itself and that of theatre is in the spectator. He goes on to say explicitly: 'Cette foule joue en quelque sorte en art dramatique l'office de la surface plane en peinture.' (This crowd plays in some way in dramatic art the function of the flat surface in painting.) At least as striking as the lack of logic is the insistence on establishing relationships between the forms of painting and theatre. Sarcey assumes that the flat surface in painting may contribute valuably to ways of understanding a dramatic realization on a three-dimensional stage, especially in the theoretical or visual *permeability* of the frame. (The word *theory*, like *theatre*, derives from the Greek θέα [*thea*], meaning a viewing; the theorist, from *theoros*, was a spectator.) Although picture frames behind the curtain were used throughout the century for *tableaux vivants*, it was not until 1880, as Meisel documents, that 'anyone thought to put a picture frame entirely around the stage.' Experiencing that final elimination of the fore-stage and framing of sce- nic tableaux led one contemporary to observe that 'the whole has the air of a picture projected on a surface,' leading to a new 'dreamy' rela- tionship between spectators and the stage.[21]

Contemporary theorists/spectators continue to imagine theatre as Heidegger would describe painting, as a 'place of disclosure.' Like Pi- randello, Bert States imagines the essence of art as art's description of itself:

> The term *action* seems to want to refer to something inside the play, an 'in- dwelling form,' a 'soul,' an 'order of events,' etc., and so the term *imitation* takes on a second character as the medium in which the work presents its representation. Could we have it both ways, prior to and concurrent with, inside and outside? I do not see why not.[22]

States's discussion of the body and soul of the theatre, a version of what Joseph Roach calls the 'complex interplay of the organic and the me- chanical,' is an extension of the position articulated by Dumas.[23] Marvin Carlson, arguing that theatre always performs and is informed by the work of memory, goes so far as to say that 'all theatrical cultures have recognized, in some form or other, this sense of something coming back in the theatre, and so the relationships between theatre and cul- tural memory are deep and complex.'[24] The *deep* and *complex* 'ghosting' (Carlson's term) is, in his own account, speculative, depending largely upon 'the mind of the spectator.' In short, permeating the discourse of the modern theatre is a notion of spirit, mind, or essence that largely disables the opposition between the mind and material reality.

Yet, as Jean-Marie Schaeffer remarks, overcoming that opposition, which characterizes a degraded or alienated reality, implies 'cogni- tive pretensions' and an evaluative judgment.[25] Art, as the realization of spirit in form, is implicitly linked to knowledge, to power, to re- demption, and, for Hegel, only in that realization is a 'true' or 'suc- cessful' work of art achieved. But what is excluded by this confusion of the evaluative and the descriptive? 'The history of painting,' remarks Samuel Beckett, 'is the history of its attempts to escape from this sense of failure.'[26] What does it mean to say, as Beckett does, that 'to be an artist is to fail'? Beckett offers not only a vital exception to the specula- tive theory but also a protest against it. 'For others the time-abolishing joys of impersonal and disinterested speculation,' says the Unnamable. 'In my head, which I am beginning to locate to my satisfaction, above and a little to the right, the sparks spirt [*sic*] and dash themselves out against the walls. And sometimes I say to myself I am in my head, it's terror makes me say it, and the longing to be in safety, surrounded on all sides by massive bone.'[27] The subversion of the structure of inside and outside, noumena and phenomena, in Beckett leads not to a rejection of surface for depth but to a rejection of art's capacity to signify anything, including itself.

Beckett will recognize flatness and audience as necessary (if not *essential*) to both painting and drama, but if the importance of these two elements is confused in *his* work, it is self-consciously so. Contrary to the 'deep eyes' that Perez attributed to Keaton, eyes in Beckett are without dimension, conflated with a flat universe: 'blank planes sheer white eye calm long last all gone from mind.'[28] Not only have both surfaces and eyes lost integrity, but also the 'successful' overcoming of the subject–object opposition is regarded, at best, with withering irony. As we are told in *How It Is* by a voice that makes Browning's theologically minded Caliban seem dignified by comparison, 'suddenly another image the last there in the mud I say it as I hear it I see me.'[29] In Beckett's drama, perhaps extending Heisenberg's uncertainty principle, the world can only be perceived as always already radically indeterminate. Hugh Kenner writes that Beckett opposes over-interpretation and describes Beckett's universe as 'permeated by mystery.'[30] I object to the metaphor of permeation. Beckett gives us many figures that seem to epitomize what Michael Fried has called an absorptive tradition. Like the nameless character in *Act Without Words*, they sit motionless in the centre of a stage, staring at their hands, at their own navels, or, like the figure in the painterly prose piece *Still*, into space.[31] *Krapp's Last Tape* concludes with a paradigmatic image: 'Krapp motionless staring before him. The tape runs on in silence.' Have these characters achieved the self-perception that Hegel calls the knowing of self-knowing? Are they seeing themselves for the first time, inwardly? That is the epistemological puzzle that Beckett seems to ask us to engage. And the conventional wisdom of critics writing very much in the Hegelian tradition is that Beckett's work is significant because he has so brilliantly combined form and content. Such an understanding is misguided. At the very least, it is difficult to reconcile with Beckett's famous comment that the modern artist must recognize that there is 'nothing to express.'[32]

In the early novel *Murphy* the protagonist plays chess with the solipsistic Mr Endon (*on* is Greek for *being*). Endon's very being, the end of being, mocks the idea of depth. His eyes are 'both deep-set and protuberant, one of Nature's jokes.'[33] He seems to play a game of chess (vibrates to Murphy's 'chessy eye'), but is, like the board on which he manipulates 'the black,' entirely two-dimensional; the pieces have no intrinsic value but simply make patterns on the surface. Only when Murphy realizes that the patterns have no significance is he able 'to see nothing, that colourlessness which is such a rare postnatal treat.' Beckett's fiction and drama manifest what Hayden White has called the 'tendency of modernist literature to dissolve the event,' and Beckett is vitally concerned with the problem of representing history; in particular, a history that cannot be adequately remembered and whose meaning cannot be unambiguously identified. The most famous instance of that failure in both structural and characterological terms is *Waiting for Godot* (1948). 'It is the anomalous nature of modernist events,' White writes, 'that undermine [*sic*] not only the status of facts in relation to events but also the status of the event in general.'[34]

The Holocaust has been described as the paradigmatic modernist event, the epitome of the unrepresentable. According to the philosopher Emil Fackenheim, the Holocaust resists historical explanations that seek causes and 'the theological kind that seeks meaning and purpose.' In short, 'one cannot comprehend [the Holocaust] but only confront and object.'[35] Beckett is centrally concerned with this problem of artistic-historical representation, the paradox that 'there is nothing to express, nothing with which to express, nothing from which to express, no power to express, no desire to express, together with the obligation to express.'[36] That problem tends to be figured, if at all, as ghostly or phantasmagoric. 'The effect of the representation,' remarks White, 'is to endow all events with spectral qualities ... The outside of events, their phenomenal aspects, and their insides, their possible meanings or significances, have been collapsed and fused. The meaning of events remains indistinguishable from their occurrence, but their occurrence is unstable, fluid, phantasmagoric.'[37]

Paradoxically, the years immediately following the Second World War were among Beckett's most prolific; he completed his trilogy of novels, *Waiting for Godot,* and several important works of art criticism between 1946 and 1950. At the same time, post-war Paris proved remarkably fruitful ground for phenomenological studies of art and the image. Maurice Merleau-Ponty and Jean-Paul Sartre are the most famous of post-war French phenomenologists, both seeking to elide the division between body and spirit, Sartre in the concept of *l'en soi* ('the in itself') and Merleau-Ponty in a theory of the subjectivity of the body.[38] Yet virtually all thinkers in this field, in a crucial historical-rhetorical shift, directly or indirectly, departed from Heidegger's 'Origin of the Work of Art' (1936), in which art had been understood as an expressive, indeed revelatory, site.[39] Beckett himself refers to current attacks on Heidegger in 'La peinture des van Velde ou le monde et le pantalon' (1948): 'Les écrits de Herr Heidegger faisaient cruellement souffrir' (the writings of Herr Heidegger have been made to suffer cruelly).[40] Heidegger argued that the art-object reveals, or speaks for, some particular subject and thus names the Being of beings. In his famous discussion of Van Gogh's painting of peasant shoes, Heidegger asked how we arrive at the essence of the work. His answer:

> ... only by bringing ourselves before Van Gogh's painting. This painting spoke. In the nearness of the work we were suddenly somewhere else than we usually tend to be.
>
> The artwork lets us know what shoes are in truth ... What happens here? What is at work in the work? Van Gogh's painting is the disclosure of what the equipment, the pair of peasant shoes, *is* in truth. The being emerges into the unconcealment of its Being.[41]

In 1948, responding in part to Heidegger's theory that art *presents* spiritual truth, Emanuel Levinas, in 'Réalité et son ombre' ('Reality and Its Shadow'), makes the ethical-ontological argument that art is radically *dégagé* or detached from reality and, hence, from responsibility. It occupies a dimension of evasion. And he seems to criticize Heidegger's non-empirical evaluation of the work of art. He challenges 'un dogme que la fonction de l'Art consiste à exprimer et que l'expression artistique repose sur une connaissance. L'artiste dit: même le peintre, même le musicien ... l'ineffable ... Là où le langage commun abdique, le poèm ou le tableau parle' (a dogma that the function of art is to express, and that artistic expression rests on a kind of knowledge. The artist tells: the painter the same as the musician ... of the ineffable ... Where common language abdicates, a poem or painting speaks).[42] On the contrary, Levinas argues, art does not *know* a particular type of reality. Art is the opposite of knowledge. The essay is clearly shaped by post-war malaise, lack of confidence in images to signify, and an almost reflexive association of images with death. In his view art obscures, like a falling of night, an invasion of shadow. Heidegger sought to discover the essence of art, the spiritual truth within art's *thingly* nature. His essay demonstrates the continued influence of the expressive theory of the Romantics: 'It is due to art's poetic essence that, in the midst of beings, art breaks open an open place, in whose openness everything is other than usual.'[43] Levinas explicitly disagrees that art casts itself towards us as what he calls '"l'être-au-monde" heideggerien' (the Heideggerian 'being-in-the-world'), arguing that the subject is in the world of things as a thing itself; it is, in short, flattened: 'Extériorité de l'intime' (an exteriority of the inmost).[44]

But, as his title alone makes clear, Levinas retains a dualistic structure, though inner and outer may be collapsed, the former, la vie intérieure represented in phantasmatic imagery (e.g., cette essence fantomatique). Reality and its shadow are to be mediated ultimately by the philosopher and critic. The problem, from Beckett's point of view, would be not only the idea that art can express anything at all, but also the notion that if art and reality are disengaged there is a space between (inter-esse) that criticism can occupy. And it is some measure of Beckett's impact on what has become a largely agnostic cultural imaginary that those theories no longer seem tenable. Derrida would later describe Heidegger's notion of truth in painting as an 'imaginary projection.' And the rhetoric of Derrida's critique of Heidegger marks the distance travelled by aesthetic theorists since 1936. 'Why always say of a painting that it renders, that it restitutes?' he asks. 'To discharge a more or less ghostly debt, restitute the shoes.'[45] But such rendering, such restitution is now impossible:

> An army of ghosts are [sic] demanding their shoes. Ghosts up in arms, an immense tide of deportees searching for their names. If you want to go to this theatre, here's the road of affect: the bottomless memory of dispossession, an expropriation, a despoilment. And there are tons of shoes piled up there, pairs mixed up and lost.[46]

The piles of shoes at Auschwitz, an image made famous in photographs and newsreels are, of course, evoked.[47] One thinks too of the pair of boots on stage as the curtain rises on the second act of Waiting for Godot: 'Estragon's boots front center, heels together, toes splayed,' but are they Estragon's? Depth in Derrida's passage is bottomless and, so, unknowable; it is not possible to be sure of internal and external coherence or intelligibility. The problem of defining a frame (or a stage set) is radical; experience cannot be comprehended.[48]

In Endgame, Clov ridicules Hamm for thinking that he 'saw inside [his] breast,' leading to what in another age would have been called a spiritual crisis. 'What's happening?' Hamm cries. But Hamm's now absurd tendency to fetishize events, to theatricalize, and, beneath it all, his desire to *recognize* in order to mourn is continually subverted. 'We're not beginning to ... to ... mean something?' he asks, wishfully. 'Mean something!' Clov famously replies. 'You and I, mean something! (*Brief laugh.*) Ah that's a good one!'[49] In 'Modern Theater Does Not Take (A) Place,' Julia Kristeva eloquently captures this sense of post-war debility: 'Since no set or interplay of sets is able to hold up any longer faced with the crises of State, religion and family, it is impossible to prefer a discourse – to play out a discourse – on the basis of a scene, sign of recognition, which would provide for the actor's and audience's recognition of themselves in the same Author.'[50] My aim, in citing Levinas, Derrida, and Kristeva, is to historicize the rhetoric of *surface, depth, frame, spectre, recognition,* even of *meaning,* and to suggest, at least in some fields of discourse, a paradigm shift in the use of those terms. For Beckett, to discuss the importance of the frame itself, the boundary by which an entity may be defined, is both pretentious and dishonest. For the frame implies a bracketed situation, a subject–object relation, and the validity of a perspective that conceals and reveals. But, as Beckett writes, 'All that should concern us is the acute and increasing anxiety of the relation itself, as though shadowed more and more darkly by a sense of invalidity.'[51] The flatness of the canvas, itself a supposed frame between the viewer and what is *within* the picture, cannot be overcome: 'For what is this coloured plane, that was not there before.' It is not simply that interior and exterior, subject and object, have lost their integrity, or that the frame has become radically ambiguous, but further, Beckett shows, it becomes absurd to discuss that which is *within*.

One modernist reaction to the theory that art has an essence to disclose, most famously articulated by Clement Greenberg, declares that depth is an illusion and that the being of art is in the thing itself. Greenberg argues that modernist painting *uniquely* orients itself to the 'ineluctable flatness of the surface.'[52] A distinguishing feature of such painting is its insistence on the artifice of its own undertaking. Despite advancing such a definition, however, Greenberg acknowledges the limits of a painting's capacity to refer exclusively to its own flatness. Thus, he discovers a new sort of perspective: a 'kind of third dimension' that is no longer a function of space but is purely optical. 'The flatness toward which Modernist painting orients itself can never be an utter flatness,' he writes. 'The heightened sensitivity of the picture plane may no longer permit sculptural illusion, or *trompe-l'oeil*, but it does

and must permit optical illusion. The first mark made on a surface destroys its virtual flatness, and the configurations of a Mondrian still
suggest a kind of third dimension.'[53] Greenberg claims that the surface
of painting takes the viewer into an illusion of depth but that depth is
not there. In short, painting lies, unless what it refers to is itself. Beckett
ultimately says, yes, art lies, but the claim is not radical enough because
art itself is a lie. You cannot deny art referentiality and then say that art
refers to itself. Beckett challenges the very being of art, yet his drama
has been interpreted as assuming what amounts to Greenberg's non-
representational, objectivist goal, although this position amounts to
little more than an extension of the Romantic form–content dialectic.
Maurice Valency, for instance, says that 'Beckett represents a very ad-
vanced stage of nineteenth-century symbolism, perhaps its terminal aspect, the point at which the symbol symbolizes only itself, and poetry
ceases to convey anything.'[54]

If being is not in the art itself, then it is in the eye of the beholder.
Beckett recognizes this position as an inevitable consequence of the
human desire for meaning. As Michael Fried would later write in
'Shape as Form: Frank Stella's New Paintings': 'The universal power
of any mark to suggest something like depth belongs not so much to
the art of painting as to the eye itself.'[55] In *Film* Beckett depicts an object fleeing from such an eye. Beginning with Berkeley's *esse est percipi,*
Beckett will show that, if the artist is honest, he will strive to avoid
not just *percipi* but also *esse*. 'Ceasing to be, I ceased to see,' says the
Unnamable. 'Delicious instant truly.'[56]

In his 1948 essay 'Peintres de l'empêchement,' Beckett had named and
admired the two positions I have attributed to Greenberg and Fried. He
called them 'l'empêchement-objet' (object-obstacle) and 'l'empêchement-
oeil' (eye-obstacle):

> ... Car que reste-t-il de représentable si l'essence de l'objet est de se dérober
> à la représentation?
> Il reste à représenter les conditions de cette dérobade. Elles prendront
> l'une ou l'autre de deux formes, selon le sujet.
> L'un [sorte d'artiste] dira: Je ne peux voir l'objet, pour le représenter,
> parce qu'il est ce qu'il est. L'autre: Je ne peux voir l'objet, pour le représenter,
> parce que je suis ce que je suis.
> [... For what remains to represent if the essence of the object evades
> representation?
> What remains to be represented are the conditions of this evasion. These
> conditions will take one of two forms according to the subject.

The one [kind of artist] will say: I cannot see the object, in order to represent it, because it is what it is. The other: I cannot see the object in order to represent it, because I am what I am.][57]

Beckett both denies art the ability to represent anything, including itself, and exposes the perceiver dramatizing himself in the act of perception. The paintings of Geer and Bram van Velde (the subjects of the essay) analyse nullity (*un état de privation*). The first kind of artist approaches privation from the outside (*du dehors*), the second from the inside (*du dedans*). Richard Begam argues that for Beckett the van Veldes 'illustrate the coming asunder of this [object–subject] dialectic,' and a turning away from conventional subject–object categories is characteristic of much of Beckett's art criticism.[58] Yet an unmistakable ambivalence in the piece, a layering of contradictions, makes it difficult to assign a philosophically consistent position to Beckett:

La résolution s'obtient chez l'un par l'abandon du poids, de la densité, de la solidité, par un déchirement de tout ce qui gâche l'espace, arrête la lumière, par l'engloutissement du dehors sous les conditions du dehors. Chez l'autre parmi les masses inébranlables d'un être écarté, enfermé et rentré pour toujours en lui-même, sans traces, sans air, cyclopéen, aux bref éclairs, aux couleurs du spectre du noir.[59]

[The resolution is obtained, in one case, by abandoning [the object as a thing of] weight, density, solidity, by casting aside all that wastes or takes up space, stops or blocks the light, by the swallowing up of the outside under the conditions of the outside. In the other, by admitting that the object is relegated to a hermit's stash, locked up and buried for always in itself, without traces, without air, cyclopean, in short flashes, in the colours of the shade of blackness.]

If we blame *res extensa* (Descartes's term for extended space) for objects' non-representability, we accuse the outside of swallowing up those things which are external to us under conditions of externality. Thus, Beckett reverses Heidegger's epiphanic notion of unconcealment, rendering those things inaccessible to representation which, presumably, would corrupt their externality by bringing them into *res cogitans* and thus effacing them in their true nature, losing them instead of representing them. On the other hand, the fault for objects' non-representability might lie within *res cogitans* itself.[60]

Yet form and content collapse upon one another in the passage, and Beckett's position, refracted through metaphor upon metaphor, is characteristically indeterminate. His *en lui-même* ought to evoke but is not equivalent to Sartre's *l'en soi*, for though it leaves no trace, being appears as the *spectre du noir*, a haunting yet purposely indefinite image (indeed, a non-image). The very notion of *résolution* that drives the passage is contradicted in the following paragraph by the sense of 'un dévoilement sans fin' (an unveiling without end). Unveiled (in another mixed metaphor) is the hard flatness of art itself, 'cellule peinte sur la pierre de la cellule,' a cell-coloured paint on the stone of the cell. In a similar, overtly purgatorial image, penned around the same time, Molloy would imagine himself 'flattened ... against a rock the same colour as myself, that is grey ... the rock in the shadow of which I crouched like Belaqua.'[61] Art does not draw attention to itself, though its medium (the paint) may be said to represent flatness of the support (the cyclopean stones of the prison wall). The paradoxical non-colour of colour, the shades of black, indicates the radical indeterminacy not only of essence but also of existence. But the overdetermined metaphor (*cellule*), the wretched sense of imprisonment by this *art d'incarcération*, asserts again the notion that interiority is the basis for the cognition of being, if not for being itself.

In his final monologue in *Endgame*, Clov seems to imagine himself as the painter-engraver whom Hamm had earlier described dragging to the window in the asylum ('I once knew a madman who thought the end of the world had come. He was a painter – and engraver'). As such, and suggesting a morbid pun in *engraver*, Clov tellingly returns to Beckett's metaphor of the cell: 'I open the door of the cell and go. I am so bowed I only see my feet, if I open my eyes, and between my legs a little trail of black dust.' In the action that follows, Clov does not, in fact, open the door and go outside. Perhaps 'the earth is extinguished, though I never saw it lit.'[62] The sense of frustration that pervades Beckett's art indicates a combination of bitterness and resignation. 'How little one is at one with oneself, good God,' complains Molloy. 'I who prided myself on being a sensible man, cold as crystal and as free from spurious depth.'[63] The non-integral one cannot think entirely outside of the Cartesian paradigm or avoid altogether a spiritual sense of selves, but imagines instead a world of contradictions: dead images, *spectres du noir*, a flat reality, a non-reflective surface that subverts or evades the specular nature of philosophical reflection. Derrida has called this surface 'the tain of the mirror,' an image with which Beckett was familiar even in 1948, when he contributed 'Peintres de l'empêchement' to the journal *Derrière le Miroir*.[64] It is to the actual surfaces, the media themselves, that we turn in the next section, to consider if, in the absence of reflection, there remains nothing to be done.

*Endgame* represents the first key figuration of the flatness of a picture in Beckett's dramatic work. The play begins with the stage directions:

> *Bare interior . . .*
> *Left and right back, high up, two small windows, curtains drawn.*
> *Front right, a door. Hanging near door, its face to wall, a picture.*

The apparent emphasis, in fact, priority, given to interiority has encouraged readings of the play as a dramatization of human consciousness. The theatrical space is the inside of a skull, and Hamm, who is located in precisely the centre of that space, frequently gives voice to the illusion of human interiority: 'There's something dripping in my head.' 'Last night I saw inside my breast.' The windows are read as eyes that implicitly draw the spectators deeper into the stage space and tempt the viewer with a seeming promise of even further interiority. But the painting immediately contradicts such a reading. The one overt reference in the play to the painter is to a man incapable of seeing in the way the windows seem to encourage. 'I used to go and see him, in the asylum,' says Hamm. 'I'd take him by the hand and drag him to the window. Look! There! All that rising corn! The sails of the herring fleet! All that loveliness! . . . He'd snatch his hand away and go back to his corner. Appalled. All he had seen was ashes.' The story may be inconclusive on the subject of visibility, perspective, and illusion. But there are few ways better to insist upon the utter flatness of the picture surface than by hanging it picture-side to the wall.

In short, Beckett moves beyond a simple schematization of windows signifying depth and the reversed painting signifying the impossibility of insight and here ironizes the painting as a metaphor itself for art. It is, of course, still recognizably a picture when it faces the wall, but the image denies what Stanton Garner sees as implicit in the visual field of Beckett's plays, namely, the animation of the creative eye, a 'modern dynamism' and a consequent 'visual poetics.'[65] One might note too that when the painting is replaced in the end by the alarm clock, Beckett teaches us to think in terms of another kind of flatness, denying, in effect, temporal perspective or dimension. In *Endgame* time has no depth, no sense of now/here, then/there. The only use made of the clock before it is hung in place of the painting has been not to tell time but to set off its deafening alarm. Hamm and Clov listen appreciatively: 'The end is terrific!' says Clov. Hamm replies, 'I prefer the middle.' To use the spatial metaphor, *Endgame* flattens time through the conjunction of clock and painting.[66]

In *Proust*, a work organized around the binary opposition of surface and depth, Beckett had explicitly described moments of temporal flatness:

> The identification of immediate with past experience, the recurrence of past action or reaction in the present, amounts to a participation between the ideal and the real, imagination and direct apprehension, symbol and substance ... What is common to present and past is more essential than either taken separately. Reality, whether approached imaginatively or empirically, remains a surface, hermetic. Imagination, applied – a priori – to what is absent, is exercised in vacuo and cannot tolerate the limits of the real ... The experience is at once imaginative and empirical.[67]

In Proust, faced with a flat reality, the imagination applies to or conjures, a priori, what is absent, in effect, giving depth to flatness. Such recognition of flatness marks exceptional, indeed mystical, moments in Proust, whose world, Beckett writes, is hoisted from a 'deep source,' by the 'diver' called 'involuntary memory.' 'The artist,' claimed the young Beckett, 'does not deal in surfaces ... because the only possible spiritual development is in the sense of depth. The artistic tendency is not expansive, but a contraction.' Beckett's art will tend towards contraction, but his aim, in contrast to what he takes to be that of Proust, will be to situate the self, as Neary in *Murphy* says of Miss Dwyer, at 'one with the ground against which she so prettily figured.' Although 'Murphy's mind *pictured itself* as a large hollow sphere, hermetically closed to the universe without,' we are told by Neary in the novel's opening pages that, in fact, 'All life is figure and ground.'[68]

There is another way to reject the illusion of perspective and to stress the flatness of a painting even more effective than turning its face to the wall. In *Film*, O [object], disturbed by a print of God the Father pinned to the wall of his room, 'tears print from wall, tears it in four, throws down the pieces and grinds them underfoot.' Three features of this action are crucial. First, the negation of an idea of art whose content is divine is an obvious response to a theological ontology that connects a sensuous to a spiritual experience of art, linking the sacred and the secular or man-made. O tears God's picture to pieces. Second, material tearing of the print implies that the being of the painting is negated with the destruction not of what the print represents but of the very flatness of the support, the paper itself. The print is also a mechanical reproduction of a painting and, itself, lacking the textured surface that is slightly less flat in the 'original' painting. And, this point leads to Beckett's brilliance in what I take to be a third crucial point; namely, that if the tearing of the print provokes questions about the medium or the physical reality of art, then the spectator in the cinema must wonder, what is film? Walter Benjamin argues that the mechanical reproduction effaces the possibility of the original, and similarly in Beckett, the tearing up of the reproduction with its concomitant implication of a destruction of God iterates in action the *only* thing that reproduction can ever accomplish in principle: the annihilation of the original.

In the case of the print in *Film*, the original may be not only painting but godhead itself. Well, we can't get to the original of God through print *or* painting because the bastard doesn't exist. Beckett seems to indicate by analogy that we can't get to the original of O either, for the same reason. But in the case of the latter the viewer can only sit, like O (perhaps also zero), and impotently contemplate flatness, in the play of light upon the screen, that is ultimate and non-representational.[69] The flatness of *Film* denies not only the presentness of a reality beyond or even *in* the surface of the silver screen but also our presentness to it. 'The screen is not a support, not like a canvas,' observes Stanley Cavell. 'There is nothing to support, that way. It holds a projection, as light as light. A screen is a barrier. What does the silver screen screen? It screens me from the world it holds – that is, makes me invisible. And it screens that world from me.'[70] An obvious feature of all movies is that audiences are never present to the performance of the actors. In this case the explicit and radical isolation of O does not lead to the Cartesian affirmation of *cogito*, but to the nothing which is that rare postnatal treat.

Set in 1929, *Film* refers to and inverts the iconography of Chaplin's *Modern Times* (Chaplin was Beckett's first choice for the role of O). The flatness of *Film* precludes the spiritual dimension of *Modern Times* that Chaplin described in Bergsonian rhetoric, when in a note he had characterized the Tramp and the Waif as 'the only two live spirits in a world of automatons. They really live. Both have an eternal spirit of youth ... We are spiritually free.'[71] The conclusion of *Film* rejects the illusion of depth epitomized by the gamine and Little Tramp's walking away from the camera down a limitless road into a sunset, substituting O rocking back and forth – moving but going nowhere. The undermining of the

myth of perspective makes strange significant relations not only between objects within the work but also between the work of art and the
spectator. O [object] and E [eye] are ultimately shown to be identical.

In representing the experience of perception, Beckett claims to encounter 'a problem of images which [he] cannot solve without technical
help.' The problem itself is that of the mobility of the perceiving eye or
consciousness. He seeks to convey the fundamental nature of the problem of self-perception. The opening directions read:

> Esse est percipi.
> All extraneous perception suppressed, animal, human, divine, self-
> perception maintains in being.
> Search of non-being in flight from extraneous perception breaking
> down in inescapability of self-perception.
> No truth value attaches to above, regarded as of merely structural and
> dramatic convenience.[72]

The problem of self-perception is conveyed through the structure of
the action. *Film* is divided into three parts, like many earlier plays
(Strindberg's *Ghost Sonata*, for instance, which Roger Blin directed and
Beckett saw at the Gaîté-Montparnasse in 1949) dealing with the problem of subjectivity, taking the central character and the viewer from
(1) the street to (2) the stairs, to (3) the room. O [object] moves, like
Strindberg's Student or like Hamlet, progressively into deeper architectural spaces. He avoids all eyes, from God's in the print to his own in a
mirror, that might confirm his own being. He covers a mirror with a rug
to avoid the reflection. But if self-perception (being) will come, even if
unsought, in the non-visible interior of the body, Beckett attaches no
truth value to it. O falls into a doze: 'E's gaze pierces the sleep, O starts
awake, stares up at E. Patch over O's left eye now seen for the first time.'
Has O been dreaming? Beckett has emphasized the 'unreal quality'
of the film already. Can one achieve self-perception in the midst of a
dream? Descartes was troubled by just such dreams. Does the patch
on his eye signify that he has been imagining vision insufficiently, as
merely physical, and that, like Oedipus, he recognizes, though partially
blind, that he can really see at last? The final image of O is dark and un-
satisfying: 'He sits, bowed forward, his head in his hands, gently rocking. Hold it as the rocking dies down.' The teleological structure that
*Film* explicitly sets out in the beginning comes to rest with the rocking
chair, though it does not completely rest, for this is a *motion* picture.

If the Romantics replaced the mirror with the lamp, Beckett denies the lamp's efficacy. 'A dim lamp was all I had been given,' complains Molloy, 'and patience without end to shine it on the empty shadows. I was a solid in the midst of other solids.'[73] In his later work, Beckett effectively moves beyond the absorption/theatricality opposition because he does not just pretend to reject the audience. He does reject it. And he rejects the Romantic theory of organic form that remains central to so much modernist art and critical theory. As Frank Kermode put it: 'Forms are the food of Faith; they are symbols of another order of truth that can never be wholly private because ... they are that complete fusion of form and meaning, spirit and body, which also characterizes the image of art.'[74] Beckett is largely bored by the Romantic optimism of modern artists such as Kandinsky, who proclaims: 'That is beautiful which is produced by internal necessity, which springs from the soul.'[75] In 'Three Dialogues,' Beckett mocks 'the artist obsessed with his expressive vocation ... and the every man his own wife experiments of the spiritual Kandinsky.'[76] Such experiments are just another instance of the same old history of painting, 'the history of its attempts to make up for this sense of failure, by means of more authentic, more ample, less exclusive relations between representer and representee.'[77] To Hamm's brutal 'Neither gone nor dead?' Clov replies for all of Beckett's characters: 'In spirit only.'[78]

The absence or death of the spirit is an epistemological and, specifically, a visual problem for Beckett. It may seem paradoxical, therefore, that ghosts figure so prominently in his oeuvre, for ghosts imply not the transcendence but the immanence of the spirit. The body dies. The spirit lives. Yet Beckett's ghostly work resists imputation of life to the Hegelian mind [*Geist*] as the desperate last gasp of the imagining (and the imaginary) subject. Beckett's being has reached a dead end (End-*on*). In 'Imagination Dead Imagine,' the second-person subject is told, 'Go back out, a plain rotunda, all white in the whiteness, go back in, rap, solid throughout ... The light that makes all so white no visible source, all shines with the same white shine, ground, wall, vault, bodies, no shadow.' The images of biologically living woman and man lying back to back on the ground are discovered. 'The bodies seem whole and in fairly good condition, to judge by the surfaces exposed to view.' But like the image, life itself has no clear source and is indistinguishable from the multiple surfaces on which it can scarcely be said to appear: 'No, life ends and no, there is nothing elsewhere.'[79] Nothing is more real than nothing. Their breaths mist the surface of a mirror, but there is no reflection of them in it. The mirror suggests not consciousness but the absence of any being other than the biological, the dead image.

Soon after making *Film*, Beckett was in Stuttgart to direct *Eh Joe* (1966) for television. Nancy Illig reports: 'Beckett came in one morning and said "Now we'll make it all dead," and this is how by progressive reduction we ended up with the hammering staccato of a ghost's voice.'[80] The flattening (hammering) of the voice is, she implies, what makes it dead. Yet the drama draws upon the old trope, the inside of a man's head. It appears to be another Cartesian drama: Alone in his room, Joe eliminates all external stimuli and listens to the voice in his head. However, the voice is not his own, and in this way Beckett subverts the paradigmatic inside-outside structure. Woman's voice: 'You know that penny farthing hell you call your mind ... That's where you think this is coming from, don't you?'[81] The question (like the refrain, 'Eh Joe?') is more than rhetorical, but no answer is given. 'Behind the eyes,' over the years, Joe has been committing murder, 'throttling the dead in his head.' What will happen when 'all your dead [are] dead' (204) and there is '[n]ot another soul to still'? The play does not simply replace the *cogito* with *cogitas* or *cogita*. Thinking itself, it becomes increasingly clear, is associated with the illusions generated by the television set and the television viewer's helpless exclusion from and by the medium. The play concludes with the voice dropping to a whisper: '[... *almost inaudible except words in italics*.] All right ... You've had the best ... Now *imagine*.'[82]

Once again, Beckett employs three movements to suggest progressively deeper states of interiority or absorption. Joe is first seen by the camera, from behind, sitting on the edge of a bed. He gets up, opens the window, and looks out. Then he closes the window. He repeats the action with a cupboard. He closes the cupboard. Then he closes his eyes. And the camera moves in towards his face. The following 'interior' monologue is interrupted briefly nine times; during each interruption the camera moves a few inches closer to Joe's face. The voice is that of a female ghost, and like the ghosts of Renaissance tragedy, she is a figure of revenge. But the play does not represent the action of a revenge drama. The play does not even represent, as Ibsen's *Ghosts*, which has an analogous final tableau, a frustrated intersubjectivity or the progressive deterioration of subjectivity. Instead, by the manipulation of camera, voiceless face, and faceless voice, *Eh Joe* depicts the fact of impenetrability figured in the fundamentally visual imperative: *Imagine*.

The association of flatness with death is a crucial feature of Beckett's short prose of the 1960s, when his own vision was seriously deteriorating.

James Knowlson argues that texts such as 'Imagination Dead Imagine' and *The Lost Ones* 'owe a lot to [Beckett's] recent work in film and television. A determined effort is made to "see" the entire structure and organization of the cylinder and to describe the workings of the "abode" as precisely as the "eye of the mind" (or as the lens of a camera) will allow.'[83] But the lost ones exist 'inside a *flattened* cylinder.'[84] The problem of vision is paradoxically both overly metaphysical and overly physical. For instance, 'None looks within himself where none can be ... They may stray unseeing through the throng indistinguishable to the eye of flesh from the still unrelenting ... They crawl blindly in the tunnels in search of nothing.'[85] Those who are sedentary 'devouring with their eyes in heads dead still each body as it passes by. Standing or sitting they cleave to the wall all but one in the arena stricken in the midst of the fevering ... Some come to rest from time to time all but the unceasing eyes.'

In his *German Diaries*, Beckett commented on Caspar David Friedrich's painting *Two Men Observing the Moon*: 'pleasant predilection for 2 tiny languid men in his landscape, that is the only kind of romantic still tolerable, the bémolisé.'[86] In a striking double entendre, Beckett employs the French musical term *bémol* (flat) to describe Friedrich's painting. One could read the remark as a mixed metaphor by which the subject of the painting is transposed to a minor key. However, such a reading would miss the synaesthetic importance of the pun – the emphasis on pictorial flatness – and Beckett's ambivalence in regard to the Romantic subject. The flatness denoted by *bémolisé* applied to Romantic painting indicates some measure of the complexity and importance of Beckett's late 'play for television,' *Ghost Trio* (1975). In a letter written in 1937, Beckett had imagined that a new literary genre could realize the 'tonal surface' of the 'large black pauses' in Beethoven's Seventh Symphony, 'connecting unfathomable abysses of silence.'[87] The title of the television play, forty years later, explicitly refers to Beethoven's piano trio in three movements, only the second of which (the *Largo*) is flattened, or in a minor key; it is that movement which gives the trio its ghostly name. The music for Beckett's *Ghost Trio* is drawn solely from the *Largo*.

*Ghost Trio* seemed to Beckett a recapitulation, in short, of all his major work. In a letter to Con Leventhal he wrote that he had 'got down first corpse of TV piece. All the old ghosts. *Godot* and *Eh Joe* over infinity. Only remains to bring it to life.'[88] Even in a note, the notion of framing, here through quantitative analysis ('over infinity'), is exploded. *Ghost Trio* may be a culmination or an extension of the ghost motif, but it is not a *re-presentation*. Beckett places his oeuvre in the context of ghost watching, and it is possible to understand ghost watching better in the context of his oeuvre. (With ... *but the clouds* ... and *Not I, Ghost Trio* was later featured in a three-part program organized by the BBC called *Shades*.) In this television drama, the 'figure' (F), another man in a room or, as we are told by a voice, 'the familiar chamber,' appears torn between the inner and the outer world. He seems drawn to thresholds, creaking open the window or the door, between the unknown without and the incommensurable privacy of his own interior. At the end of the third movement a boy comes to him, perhaps the same as came to Vladimir at the end of *Waiting for Godot*, with the same bad news.

> *Cut to near shot of small boy full length in corridor before the open door. Dressed in black oilskin with hood glistening with rain. White face raised to invisible F. 5 seconds. Boy shakes head faintly. Face still, raised. 5 seconds. Boy shakes head again. Face still, raised. 5 seconds. Boy turns and goes. Sound of receding steps. Register from the same position his slow recession till he vanishes in the dark at end of corridor. 5 seconds on empty corridor.*[89]

The ghost, it appears, like Godot before her, will not appear tonight, except as depicted renunciation, postponement, or denial. The rain on the boy's oilskin suggests a distinct outside with a different environment from that of the inside. The slow recession and long view of the corridor obviously represent depth and perspective. But, to quote the female voice (V), which, like that in *Eh Joe*, radically complicates the Cartesian *me cogitare*, 'Forgive my stating the obvious. [*Pause.*] ... Now look closer. [*Pause.*] Floor.'

Contained in a box smaller than a stage, indeed closer in size to the head of an individual spectator, the television drama gives the illusion of a more private space than that of any theatre. The 'small box,' Enoch Brater remarks, 'is a more congenial metaphor [than the movie screen] for being inside someone's head.'[90] The spectator's vision is entirely shaped by both the limitations and the mobility of a camera that, as Beckett made explicit in *Film*, is not just a prosthetic but a pretend eye. Here too the camera has three positions (labelled A, B, C) that mark a progression inward. Brater argues that in the television dramas 'Beckett poeticizes the story of a mind turned inward upon itself ... The great emphasis placed on repeated images allows us to discover the hidden poetry in the poorest objects ... the human quality located in the images themselves.' But Beckett again challenges the notion that an object or event can have an observable meaning, that the selection of *important* details can be anything but arbitrary and, consequently, that the framing or structuring of an action can indicate anything but its own evanescence. This television drama, in 1975, is an astonishingly subtle treatment of, among other things, the problematic status of the medium itself. Despite the precision and repetition made possible by the technology, the television camera cannot, as Michael Turits wrote of media coverage of the 1986 NASA *Challenger* space shuttle disaster, 'reconstruct the too brief event as a visually intelligible event.'[91] Beckett had anticipated this problem in *Murphy* fifty years earlier when Neary had pictured Miss Dwyer: 'The face ... or system of faces, against the big blooming confusion.'[92] *Ghost Trio* does not present the viewer with the realism that one expects of the conventional television drama, though it has elements of the living-room set, with its exterior door stage right. Furthermore, the technological innovation of television's capacity to replay from different camera angles does not clarify or define the action. The drama presents us not with the essence of the object or event but with the conditions of evasion.

Returning to concepts articulated in 'Peintres de l'empêchement,' *Ghost Trio* evokes both the outside swallowed up under conditions of the outside and the inside 'locked up and buried for always in itself, without traces, without air, cyclopean, in short flashes, in the colours of the shade of blackness.'[93] The spectator is not simply given the 'familiar chamber,' but instructed in a mode of looking. After the initial fade up to a general view of the room which lasts ten seconds, the invisible V delivers the following flat monologue:

> Good evening. Mine is a faint voice. Kindly tune in accordingly. [*Pause.*] Mine is a faint voice. Kindly tune in accordingly. [*Pause.*] It will not be raised, nor lowered, whatever happens. [*Pause.*] Look. [*Long pause.*] The familiar chamber. [*Pause.*] On the right the indispensable door. [*Pause.*] On the left, against the wall, some kind of pallet. [*Pause.*] The light: faint omnipresent. No visible source. As if luminous. Faintly luminous. No shadow. [*Pause.*] No shadow. Colour: none. All grey. Shades of grey. [*Pause.*] The colour grey if you wish, shades of the colour grey. [*Pause.*] Forgive my stating the obvious. [*Pause.*] Keep that sound down. [*Pause.*] Now look closer. [*Pause.*] Floor.[94]

This opening (and only) monologue is both disconnected from the embodied figure who is seen, and concerned centrally with defining the space of the action and its boundaries, the conditions of vision, and the ghostly indeterminacy of lighting and shade. Yet each close-up, of floor, wall, door, window ('an opaque sheet of glass'), pallet, is the same: '*Smooth grey rectangle 0.70 m. × 1.50 m.* [or, in one slight variation, *2 m.*].' V insists on the identity not only of every surface but also of every image: 'Having seen that specimen of floor you have seen it all. Wall.' Thus, the 'obvious' is only obviously ironic if we fail to recognize the tendency to see what is not there, the impulse to *imagine*. Shades that admit no distinction give way to images of flatness. And every surface provokes the radical problem of what it means *to know*: 'Knowing this, the kind of wall ... the kind of floor ... Look again ... Door ... Window.' These instructions, with the instant replay enabled by the television camera, are repeated until the movement ends with an evocation of so many of Beckett's figures, but specifically of Krapp; the camera moves in on the seated figure, 'head bowed,' clutching a cassette.

The figure is apparently waiting for a ghost, but he also has ghostly qualities himself. If the outer world, from which visual and aural images may come, is radically uncertain, so is the inner world, the mental tableau. Both the room and F are composed of opaque, non-reflective surfaces. To suggest an analogy between the room and the self, the drama compels the spectator to change perspectives. The second movement opens with the 'voice's' indeterminate instruction: 'He will now think he hears her.' The voice has shifted from the second person (in the first act) to the third, indicating a further degree of alienation from F. It is impossible for the spectator to verify that F, in fact, hears anything. V's indeterminacy undermines the metaphor of interiority, just as Molloy had commented: 'Every time I say, I said this, or I said that, or speak of a voice saying, far away inside me, Molloy, and then a fine phrase more or less clear and simple, or find myself compelled to attribute to others more or less articulate sounds, I am merely complying with the convention that demands you either lie or hold your peace.'[95]

Richard Begam makes a Derridean argument about *Molloy* that may contribute valuably to our reading of *Ghost Trio*. Self-reflection or self-mirroring, he suggests, implies an identity between subject and object, but pure consciousness eludes our cognitive grasp. There is no 'original'; the object is always already a mirrored image. Thus, in *Molloy* (which is structured on dual narratives) inside becomes outside. Begam notes Beckett's frequent interest in the 'dark glass' motif of 1 Corinthians 13 ('For now we see through a glass, darkly; but then face to face: now I know in part; but then I shall know even as also I am known'), a glass in which 'we observe ourselves to be identical yet different.'[96] The 'dark glass' epitomizes *différance*, in Begam's view, a 'principle of opposition and identity,' or what he elsewhere calls a 'radical liminality.' Yet the Derridean reading may be overextended. Does Molloy, or does F, exist *inter-esse*? Is F, on the other hand, like Endon, a solipsist? I propose a simpler reading of the mirror image in *Molloy* and *Ghost Trio*, one that denies any space-between and, instead, undermines subjectivity by asserting a kind of radical positivism, if not Protestantism. The second narrator in *Molloy*, Moran, tells us: 'I lay down and looked at my reflection, then I washed my face and hands. I waited for my image to come back, I watched it as it trembled towards an ever increasing likeness. Now and then a drop, falling from my face, shattered it again. I did not see a soul all day.'[97] Here the tenuous, unstable image appears on the surface of the water; the face is on the water and the water is on the face. Yet in a playful insertion of the idiom ('I did not see a soul all day'), depth and the self are simultaneously denied; here we recognize what Cavell calls Beckett's 'hidden literality.' What is presented is not the end of a dialectic but a rejection of the dialectical imagination altogether.

F seems torn between static self-absorption and the exterior, if no less imaginary, world of interpersonal action (e.g., when he thinks he hears her, F 'raises head sharply'). Knowlson claims that the figure is 'poised midway between two worlds.'[98] The insufficiency of this reading is indicated by the mirror that appears in the second and third movements of *Ghost Trio*, a 'small grey rectangle ... against larger rectangle of wall.' The stage directions instruct: 'close-up of mirror reflecting nothing.'[99]

The repeated trips to the margins of the visible space, to the door and window, with the dramatic enhancement of dynamic shifts in Beethoven's sonata, which is playing all the while, are increasingly indeterminate and frustrating:

> III.8. [a refrain of the action from II.10] *Crescendo creak of door opening. Near shot ... of stool, cassette, F with right ear to door. 5 seconds.*
>
> III.9. *Cut to view of corridor seen from door ... Far end in darkness. 5 seconds.*
>
> III.10. *Cut back to near shot ... of stool, cassette, F standing irresolute, door. 5 seconds.*[100]

Finally the knock comes faintly, and a boy appears whose black oilskin glistens with rain, vividly evoking the exterior but invisible world. He faintly shakes his head and departs, and the camera pans back to the figure. Has he achieved some recognition? Is he resigned? Or will he, like Vladimir, perform the same fruitless actions again tomorrow?

It is crucial to guard against totalizing claims about Beckett. As Beckett himself had written of Joyce, 'His position is in no way a philosophical one,' though it may be better understood in relation to the writings of philosophers.[101] After all, if he rejects key aspects of Romantic philosophy, he is also deeply indebted to Romantic philosophers, painters, and composers. A radical ambivalence pervades his oeuvre, built, as it is, upon the quicksand of constant epistemological anxiety and disappointment. Confronted by an unforgivingly flat world, we persist in imagining important depths: 'Seen from below the wall presents an unbroken surface all the way round and up the ceiling. And yet its upper half is riddled with niches. This paradox is explained by the levelling effect of the dim omnipresent light.'[102] The key words in this passage are 'riddled,' 'paradox,' and 'levelling.' The first returns us to Oedipus, the great riddle-solver, who goes blind but learns to know himself. The 'paradox' is not apparent but, in being asserted by the eerily objective (even scientific) narrator, comes into being as a problem of perception. And 'levelling' is again a visual reality, caused by the grey half-light. Figures are 'aghast at such depths of opacity,' to capture the paradox most succinctly.[103] Impelled to imagine but tormented by imagination, Beckett's characters, like O in *Film*, cleave to the surfaces of buildings and of rooms; the lost ones 'flatten themselves as best they can with their backs to the wall.'[104]

Finally, in the briefest possible terms, I will expand the historical scope of this discussion to describe Beckett's interest in flatness and in ghosts not only in relation to the post-war period or to modernism but also to modernity, a context that Beckett himself establishes in his first non-juvenile published work, 'Dante ... Bruno .. Vico . Joyce' (1929). The metaphor of the mirror, the ghost as a figure for the theatre, and the problem of representing interiority naturally suggest a wide range of intellectual indebtedness from *Hamlet* to *Ghosts* and from Descartes to Bergson. But, in Beckett, their prevalence indicates the limits of the possible, the murder of poetry by its own past strength, in short, the 'anxiety of influence.'[105] Further, a peculiar vehemence in Beckett about God's non-being ('The bastard! He doesn't exist,' in *Endgame*)[106] must be related to a near obsession, inspired by a life-long love of Dante, with the trope of purgatory.

Having grown up in what, for the twentieth century, has been a uniquely contested zone of Catholic and Protestant imaginaries, the world of modern Ireland, Beckett clearly responds, like other Irish writers, to his experience of what Seamus Deane calls 'a phantasmal place, inhabited by the swirling souls of the dead.'[107] Historically, Ireland has had a special, and specifically a self-reflexively poetic, relationship to purgatory. The haunting of Ireland in *Ulysses* is defamiliarized through the eyes of the Jew, Bloom, who nonetheless recognizes, implicitly, a connection between modern Dublin and purgatory, reflecting at the funeral of Paddy Dignam: 'We are praying now for the repose of his soul. Hoping you're well and not in hell. Nice change of air. Out of the fryingpan of life into the fire of purgatory.'[108] The entrance to purgatory is said to have been discovered in Ireland by Saint Patrick, who is patron saint of both Ireland and purgatory. Citing 'Shades of the Sabine farm / On the beds of St Patrick's Purgatory,' in *Station Island*, Seamus Heaney, like Yeats in his short play *Purgatory* (1939), also imagines temporal Ireland in terms of spiritual purgation and passage. In contrast to writers of both faiths, Beckett, although disillusioned with his mother's fierce Protestantism, ultimately presents a remarkable apogee of what must be called a Protestant scepticism about the image.

Beckett's discussion of the anthropologist and philosopher of history Giambattista Vico creates a genealogy from the *Scienza nuova* (new science), a rational-empirical treatment of the functions of poetry and myth (indeed, 'all things ultimately identified with God'), to what he calls the 'purgatorial' work of Joyce. Vico, Beckett argues, rejected the 'poetic spirit ... Poetry is essentially the antithesis of Metaphysics: Metaphysics purge the mind of the senses and cultivate the disembodiment of the spiritual.' In Joyce's work, the argument continues, form *is* content, and, in this sense, Joyce's work is purgatorial: 'In the absolute absence of the Absolute. Hell is lifelessness of unrelieved viciousness. Paradise the static lifelessness of unrelieved immaculation. Purgatory a flood of movement and vitality released by the conjunction of these two elements. There is a continuous purgatorial process at work, in the sense that the vicious cycle of humanity is being achieved.'[109] In this immature, if brilliant, essay Beckett articulates the central problem that his later work will strive not exactly to overcome but, rather, to undo. After imagining the perfect union of form and content in Joyce, Beckett will despair. Joyce's 'writing is not *about* something; *it is that something itself*'; Beckett's work aims to be, like the shredded picture, *nothing*. That is, not to be.

As Stephen Greenblatt has argued of early modern Protestants in his astonishing work *Hamlet in Purgatory*,

Protestants struggled ... to undo the purgatorial imagination. Only by taking the great fable apart, piece by piece, could they hope to liberate people
from it ... The easiest part of the task was to destroy the images: manuscripts
were torn up, altarpieces were disassembled and burned, sculpted images
of souls praying in the flames were smashed. Or if the images were not destroyed, they were detached gently or violently from their original meaning ... Images are vivid but vulnerable. The harder part of the zealots' task
was to chisel away a set of powerful stories, for it was in narrative even more
than in pictures that the purgatorial poem was created and maintained.[110]

An extreme version of this radical Protestant strategy informs Beckett's
earliest work. The central figure of his first short story, the quasi-
theological 'Assumption' (1929), alone in his room, 'died and was God,
each night revived and was torn, torn.'[111] For the student of Beckett, it
is impossible to read Protestant polemics of the Renaissance and not
think of O, in *Film*, tearing to pieces the print of God the Father or,
for that matter, the photographs of individuals each of whom, according
to conventional wisdom, has inherent worth. In 'A Piece of Monologue'
there is a similar tearing; the 'piece' itself is an instance of that tearing.
A ghostly speaker, barely visible upon the stage, describes the reality
of yet another man in a room: 'Backs away to edge of light and stands
facing blank wall. Covered with pictures once. Pictures of ... he all but
said of loved ones. Unframed. Unglazed. Pinned to the wall with drawing pins. All shapes and sizes. Down one after another. Gone. Torn to
shreds and scattered. Strewn all over the floor ... Nothing on the wall
now but the pins ... Nothing to be seen anywhere.' Language, like the
image, is a surface that mocks the expression of ghosts. To be dead is to
be gone: 'Ghost ... he all but said ghost loved ones. Waiting on the rip
word ... Never but the one matter. The dead and gone.'[112] Beckett un-
does what may be taken as an inadequacy of Protestant poetics and theology, specifically of the metaphysical poets, which restores the Word
of God to the central place in Christian worship but fails to recognize in
the word a danger of idolatry no less than that in the image. The 'spirit,'
in effect, is inseparable from the black ink of the material word (that is, a
'*spectre du noir*'), just as the Reformation is inseparable from the invention of the printing press. The word, like the image, is flat, a *thing of
nothing* that can be torn as easily as the page.

For that *matter*, in *Molloy*, Moran's shattering of his own image in
the pool of water, with the remark 'didn't see a soul all day,' represents not only Beckett's rejection of a theologically inflected metaphor

in Corinthians but also of Joyce's purgatorial prose. In *Ulysses* Bloom had contemplated the rock on which Nausicaa revealed herself to him: 'Tide comes here. Saw a pool near her foot. Bend, see my face there, dark mirror, breathe on it, stirs. All these rocks with lines and scars and letters. O, those transparent! . . . What is the meaning of that other world.'[113] In *Molloy* Beckett evokes this passage ironically. Opacity, not transparency, and meaninglessness compel scepticism about the very status of spirituality, of interior monologue, in short, of consciousness itself. Molloy ironizes a symbolic mode that assumes spiritual movement through (or between) states of being, as in Cocteau's *Orphée* (1949), in which the dead pass through watery mirrors. Protestants, of course, did not disbelieve in a theologically ordered universe or, for that matter, in the life of the spirit. What they sought to undo was a poetics that supported, in their view, an insidious institutional structure. Beckett's protest is far more extreme. Purgatory is a middle space, between heaven and hell, between life and final rest, but in Beckett's flattened universe liminality is a cruel joke. There can be neither overcoming (*aufheben*) nor *différance* in this *état de privation*. In *Malone Dies*, Macmann remarks, 'I have pinned my faith to appearances, believing them to be vain.'[114]

When the Bible is mentioned in *En attendant Godot*, it is remembered by Estragon, who admits to having been a poet, as a picture book with vivid colours, not as the revelatory text Vladimir would have it be. Did Gogo see it at 'l'école sans Dieu' (the school without God)? He replies, 'Sais pas si elle était sans ou avec' (I don't know if it was without or with).[115] But it is in *Endgame* that Christian pictorialism is most brilliantly acknowledged and renounced in terms of the stage, again in the juxtaposition of the painting that faces the wall and the two curtained windows. When Beckett was writing *Fin de partie* in 1956 he was also rereading the complete plays of Racine, plays that he had taught at Trinity College years earlier. Racine was going through a major revival in the 1950s, culminating in a new edition of his plays published in 1960. In his own contribution to that revival, Roland Barthes commented on Racine's contemporaneity, remarking that 'the French author most frequently associated with the idea of a classical *transparence* is the only one to have made all the new languages of the century converge upon himself.'[116] Barthes goes on to acknowledge that 'transparence is an ambiguous value; it is both what cannot be discussed and what there is most to say about.' It is just such a paradoxical transparency to which Beckett's opacity so powerfully responds.

Of all the past literature to which Beckett's play speaks, none is as directly relevant in the present context as Racine's final play, *Athalie*, in which a High Priest and his stepson inhabit the inner sanctum of the Temple of Jerusalem. It is yet another play (as Barthes also notes) built on the tripartite architectural structure of ever deeper interiors (exterior, ante-chamber, chamber). Like *Endgame, Athalie* involves both heightened rhetorical performance and brutality. The context is a world steeped in blood, a race extinguished ('éteindre la race,' 1.1.95), as in *Fin de partie* the lights of those who once lived outside the shelter have been 'éteinte[s] [extinguished].'[117] Racine's play about the Kingdom of Israel, however, is written in praise of God. It builds to a climactic image, a revelatory tableau, when Joad, the High Priest, pulls the curtain ('Le rideau se tire' [5.5.17–18]) to disclose the young boy, Joas, descendent of David and ancestor of Jesus. Beckett's play about ending begins as Clov 'tire le rideau.' But here pulling the curtain does not reveal a pentacostal vision. To the audience, as to Hamm, the window reveals nothing. At the end of the play, apparently gazing through the window at an invisible perspective, Clov claims to see 'a small ... boy,' 'a potential procreator.' But why should we place our faith in such a vision? It is only when Hamm has a pee that Clov has been able to say with any conviction, 'Ah that's the spirit, that's the spirit!'[118] Beckett disparages, or at least teases, the common impulse to see *depth* in art, to project or even speculate about the invisible. For not only is the visual world flat, but so is the eye and the 'I.' There is nothing to express yet the obligation to express. Beckett sees nothing at all, yet all that is he sees.

# 4  The Spirit of Toys: Resurrection, Redemption, and Consumption in *Toy Story*, *Toy Story 2*, and Beyond

The overriding desire of most children is to get at and *see the soul* of their toys, some at the end of a certain period of use, others *straightaway*. It is on the more or less swift invasion of this desire that depends the length of life of a toy. I do not find it in me to blame this infantile mania; it is a first metaphysical tendency. When this desire has implanted itself in the child's cerebral marrow, it fills his fingers and nails with an extraordinary agility and strength. The child twists and turns his toy, scratches it, shakes it, bumps it against the walls, throws it on the ground . . . ; at last he opens it up, he is the stronger. But *where is the soul?* This is the beginning of melancholy and gloom.

Baudelaire, 'A Philosophy of Toys'

To infinity and beyond!

Buzz Lightyear

The history of 'seeing things' that I have described so far, from Shakespeare to Beckett, has illustrated significant changes in the relation of modern selves to the material reality of things. In the contemporary context of the computer-animated *Toy Story* movies, things seem to take on a life of their own. They have become both the stuff of identity and completely dematerialized, collapsing *res extensa* and *res cogitans*. As digital creations, theirs is a virtual reality, without even the trace of an image on celluloid, though in spin-off forms they are also more – or less – than digital. Representing this conundrum of thing-ness and immateriality, these movies extend and comment upon what Beckett perceived as 'flatness endless.' But rather than lamenting the perception that the toys' spirit is a fiction or a dream, they adapt it to an American rhetoric of self-renewal, celebrate it, and literally profit by it. Beckett's characters yearn, but fail, to end, turning ever inward (or so it appears). The toys, however, turn insistently outward – that is the only direction they *can* turn – to beseech the consumer's gaze. By virtue of their self-reflexive participation in this perpetually renewing visual economy, they become *more* real than the human spectator. For the *Toy Story* franchise, by which I mean not only the Disney-owned series of movies but also the merchandise, action figures, theme-park rides, and so on, nothing could be worse than being finished.

*Toy Story* and its sequels *Toy Story 2* and the 3D *Toy Story 3* ('The Great Escape') are deeply invested (thematically and – need it be said? – financially) in the mortality of toys. In all the movies toys come to life when human beings are not looking, though they depend on human eyes, both inside and outside the movies, for the resurrection that will enable them to survive 'to infinity and beyond.' The toys represent lives that are not only intelligent, emotional, and psychological, but also at least partially biological (as in the need to breathe oxygenated air and, it seems, the desire for physical love). And there is nothing new in dolls that drink and urinate, or puppets that fight and fuck.[1] Most important, *these* toys come to life in a way that is metaphysical. They experience a metaphysical or even a spiritual dimension in the sense that something infinite emerges from the man-made or concrete. They dream. They have imaginations. In particular, like human beings, they can and do imagine death. Their life and death, moreover, are inseparable from the medium in which they are represented.

Death is imagined obsessively in all three movies. I will focus on the first two and, particularly, on the second, which reflects with special emphasis on its status as sequel. In *Toy Story*, Death stalks in the form of an eight-year-old neighbour named Sid who wears a black T-shirt with a skull printed on it that disturbingly resembles his own face. Sid is a toy-sadist. 'He tortures toys for fun,' wails the Dinosaur Rex. He performs hideous 'medical' experiments, loves explosives, and has a pathologically violent temper. Sid's house is suburban gothic, a dark underworld of violence in the land of white picket fences. In his demolition area of a backyard Sid blows up action figures and wreaks havoc, bellowing with angry laughter. His ferocious pit-bull Skud is his sole companion. Inside his dark, bolted room, neglected by his parents, he dismembers dolls, dinosaurs, and Erector Sets. As the Disney website tells us, 'Deep within the inner sanctum of ... Sid's room, lies a collection of toys that no boy should have created. Where Andy's room is a haven for Woody [a vintage cowboy doll], Buzz [a space-ranger action figure], and all the other toys, Sid's room is no-man's-land – the work of an unwell mind.'[2]

Distinctions between *well* and *unwell, should* and *shouldn't, haven* and *no-man's-land,* are, of course, ideological; they reflect a particular set of interests and assumptions. The movies do not analyse these assumptions or offer alternative conceptual forms to those that shape and are shaped by middle-class American popular culture. Oppositions, such as that between Andy's room and Sid's, define each other. They occur within the same totalistic bipolar system, and any search for meaning within that system will be endless and self-enclosed. However, problems are raised or a drama of self-reflection occurs in the toys when they are displaced *between* social and rhetorical opposites. So, movements from Andy's room to Sid's 'no-man's-land,' from the *well* to the *unwell* (and back again) entail an experience of liminality that is crucial to experiences that may be understood as rites of passage. 'Such rites,' anthropologist Victor Turner explains, 'characteristically begin with ritual metaphors of killing or death marking the separation of the subject from ordinary secular relationships ... and conclude with a symbolic rebirth or reincorporation into society as shaped by the law and moral code.'[3] While it is not unusual for children's literature to depict such rites of passage, in these Pixar–Disney movies the 'humanity' of those undergoing the rites is radically compromised by ambiguities of origins and ends and by the extremity or pervasiveness of the capitalist world view that underlies all forms of apparent subjectivity.

That world view and the plots of the movies are inextricable from the economic histories of the companies that manufactured them. To be more precise about corporate labels: the *Toy Story* movies are produced and distributed by Pixar and Disney. Pixar was founded by John Lasseter, who left an animation job at Disney in 1984 (where he worked on *Mickey's Christmas Carol,* among other things). He then joined the filmmaker George Lucas's special-effects computer group, a division that became Pixar after being purchased in 1986 by Steve Jobs. A key artistic turning point for Lasseter was the discovery in the early 1980s that new computer-generated graphics could enhance the perception of depth in animation, well beyond what the multi-plane camera or parallax process used in traditional animation could do. Furthermore, of particular relevance to the argument I advance below is the fact that Pixar specialized in making television commercials and corporate logos. The first *Toy Story* movie (1995) was produced by Pixar and distributed by

Disney. In 1997 Pixar and Disney entered a new agreement to jointly produce five movies, one of which was *Toy Story 2*. By the terms of their revised contract, characters created by Pixar for their films were owned by Disney.[4]

Andy's toy Buzz Lightyear is a space-ranger action figure that literally falls from one property, Andy's, to another, Sid's. It will be a fortunate fall, a coming to knowledge. Buzz comes to know who he really is (He is a toy!) by learning that he cannot actually fly. Sid serves as a means to that end, not only in forcing recognition of personal limitation (Buzz can't fly), but also in representing the annihilation of self. As a character in and of himself, Sid is a cipher. Baudelaire wonders about the mysterious motives of pathologically destructive children. 'Are they,' he asks, 'in a superstitious passion against these tiny objects which imitate humanity?'('Sont-ils pris d'une colère superstitieuse contre ces menus objets qui imitent l'humanité?')[5] Sid's motivation is of little or no interest in *Toy Story*; he is a figure for terror and destruction. He is the black-cloaked alternative to his cheerful neighbour. And while Andy performs his own casual, happy violence on his toys, Andy's character also is of no interest. Instead, it is the humanity of the toys that the movie investigates. What constitutes that humanity besides the fear of death?

The inorganic material of which the toys are supposedly made ('supposedly' in that they are actually composed only of pixels and light) acquires anthropomorphic features – speech, glance, personality – from the supposed humanity of the owners. But the toys are, in fact, more 'real,' in this computer-generated movie, than the human beings who possess them. Their own putative humanity is a sort of prosthetic extension.[6] They do what Andy apparently cannot, reflect upon their own artificiality. 'A commodity appears at first sight an extremely obvious, trivial thing,' Marx writes in *Capital*. 'But its analysis brings out that it is a very strange thing, abounding in metaphysical subtleties and theological niceties.' Emphasizing the physiological basis of vision, Marx notes that these niceties can be found, not in the light that is transmitted from the external object to the eye, but in the 'misty realm of religion. There the products of the human brain appear as autonomous figures endowed with a life of their own, which enter into relations both with each other and with the human race.'[7] Apparently made of dead matter (plastic and chemicals), these toys enact a fantasy of continual resurrection, an idealizing revival of the dead, not only in the games of an individual child but also in the processes of production and marketing, of which both movies are highly self-conscious. Walter Benjamin's definition of aura, which withers in the age of mechanical reproduction, as the ability of the inanimate object to return the human gaze, suggests such an idealizing of humanity in the phantasmagoric return of toys.[8]

The climactic scene of Toy Story is a resurrection scene, clearly a spoof of those horror films in which grotesquely disfigured zombies emerge from the earth to terrify the living. This return of the living dead is not a bizarre anomaly in Toy Story, though gothic tropes are most pronounced here. The movie is replete with toys that not only come alive but also return to life. When we first see them in the opening credits, the toys appear lifeless and passive, as Andy manipulates them, inventing games, before tearing through the house with his favourite, Woody, whose arms and legs flap helplessly as Andy shakes him up and down. The frequent, even eerie, close-ups of the doll's unblinking eyes are belied, however, in a 'point-of-view-shot' – a Woody's-eye-view of Andy and Mom preparing the birthday party – that suggests a consciousness behind the painted face. After he has been dropped on Andy's bed, where he lies for a few seconds in silence, Woody first comes alive for us with a blink of the eyes. The viewer imagines that, since there are no people in it, the room is vacant. But when Woody sits up and calls to the other toys to come out, there is a pause, and the camera draws back for a deep focus so that we give our attention not to any one object but to the larger space. The room comes to life, and with it the viewer has a sense of the incompleteness of his or her own vision.

The birthday party, which follows shortly after these credits, foreshadows the later awakening of the dead in Sid's backyard. A celebration of origin and repetition, the birthday party serves to frame Toy Story, which concludes with another, explicitly religious birthday celebration, Christmas, which has a resurrection inscribed within it, and the Christ motif pervades both movies. During the first party, fearful that Andy will receive as a birthday present a new toy that will displace members of the current menagerie from his affections, Woody, the leader of the toys, sends an army of green plastic soldiers downstairs on a reconnaissance mission (an act repeated symmetrically at Christmas). When one of the 'men' is stepped on by Andy's mother, he moans, 'Go on without me,' but the sergeant hauls him up ('A good soldier never leaves a man behind'), and the soldier recovers, fixed up by a toy medic. In Sid's room, mutant toys, whom Woody takes for cannibals, fulfil a similar nursing function for the damaged and mutilated.

These acts of repair not only prefigure but also are a form of resurrection. Indeed, maimed soldier dolls appear uncannily in the resurrection scene behind Sid's house. That is, though the toys are disfigured by their owners, their inner life or essence is untouched. Toys are continually being repaired. This idea of repair as a making 'just like new' will be the major theme of the sequel. What will it mean to be *like new*?

*Toy Story 2*, though it contains no gothic subplot, picks up on the theme of resurrection in its crucial opening sequence and, as a sequel, is highly self-conscious of its own *revenant* status. The first chapter of *Toy Story 2* brilliantly encapsulates the major themes of the rest of the movie.[9] It opens in outer space, a frontier, an image of limitlessness. Slowly a figure appears hurtling into view from the depths of the galaxy, speeding, like a white-hot comet, for an alien planet. It is Buzz Lightyear. Where does he come from? We never learn. For Buzz, the destination (concrete or abstract – 'To infinity and beyond') seems more important than the origin. It will become clear, however, that origins for Buzz are to be sought in ends. His current mission, it gradually emerges, is to find, enter, and destroy the command centre of his arch-nemesis Zurg: he must find the 'Source of Zurg's Power.' Since it later turns out that Zurg (in a wink to *Star Wars* and a further teasing of the problem of originality) is Buzz's father, the source of Zurg's power is, in effect, the source of Buzz himself. Buzz lands upon the planet's surface, only to be set upon, faster than the speed of light (or vision), by an army of robots as numerous as grains of sands and spreading beyond the boundaries of the screen. He dives to the ground and sends a laser beam through a giant prism.

The refraction of the beam through the prism is a metaphor for the reproduction of images on the screen. It is an analogy and even a sort of explanation (since there must be a beam for every figure) for the countless identical images of the army of robots, which are made and destroyed by the same logic of light. (The multiplication of that potent light beam may also evoke the potentially unlimited *Toy Stories* beamed onto movie screens all over the world, suggesting perhaps that audience members are imagined by Disney to be like the robots, an infinite army of empty-headed homunculi, waiting to be overcome by a shaft of light.) Buzz blows up his enemies and finds himself hurtling onto what becomes the entrance of Zurg's fortress. An animated mechanical eyeball, another instance of the crucial optical motif, emerges from a rock face, presumably to send Buzz's image to the brain centre of the fortress, but Buzz destroys it too with his laser. The ground beneath his feet begins to tremble, as a giant, mechanical Z (for Zurg) opens, and Buzz drops down into a subterranean passageway. That Z is the last letter of the alphabet is not insignificant, since Zurg represents, in several senses, Buzz's end as well as his beginning. Letters (and spelling) are emblematic in the movie of the literacy that is explicitly imagined as both a beginning of power and a (dead) end for the many pre-literate viewers. Much of the movie's printed matter functions as *bilderverboten* (e.g., 'No Children Allowed,' a text I was always required to read aloud to my own toddler). The movie's self-reflexive intertextuality (it recalls 'No Dogs Allowed' in *Snoopy, Come Home*) becomes a further instance of the problem of origins and ends. And the viewer, like Buzz on the giant Z, always does enter the visual space that was first declared *verboten*.[10]

Underground, Buzz runs to the heart of the fortress, which is, we see a moment later, itself on a screen, a kind of panopticon inside the command post, watched by Zurg himself. The levels of spectatorship continue to multiply. 'Come to me, my prey,' Zurg chuckles demonically as he watches a little red dot (a representation of Buzz in light) blink towards the centre of his Z. Buzz approaches what seems to be the absolute centre of the fortress in the form not of Z but of O; he falls through a circular moat of vast space surrounding the source of power. Uttering his famous slogan ('To infinity and beyond!'), he presses the button on his antigravity belt and flies not to infinity but to the source, a circular platform not only in the exact centre of Zurg's fortress but also, it appears, in the middle of space itself. There, hovering in a shaft of light, is a slowly turning battery with the words 'Source of Zurg's Power' printed on it. Buzz approaches cautiously and reaches out to grasp this Holy Grail. But his hand passes through the image. It is a hologram – an illusion. The heart of the O is an absence. (It is also a text, to which I shall return.) Zurg then rises from a trapdoor in the floor behind Buzz. The 'final' combat begins, and Buzz nimbly leaps around the giant black figure of Zurg until, to the surprise and even shock of the viewer, Zurg blows him away with a laser blast. The knees of the lifeless Buzz buckle. He is dead.

The camera, which is only a visual conceit, as the video game is, draws back, and we see that we have been watching not the movie we imagined (not only the movie on a screen) but a television, on which now blink the words 'Game Over.' The movie presents the illusion of the encryption of one medium within another (a video game within a movie).[11] Pixar chose to animate *Toy Story* using shots that stayed within the bounds of what real cameras could do, even imitating live-action directors' shots.[12] In fact, since all of the represented images are digitally animated, 'camera' is really a misnomer. As Rebecca Comay remarks, 'The digitalization of storage [as opposed to an archive of film] seems to suggest a homogenization and immediate interconvert-ibility of every medium into every other.'[13] Indeed, the ontology of the 'toys' of *Toy Story* is the most serious question raised by their 'original' appearance as digitally animated figures who have already been imag-ined in diverse other media (even within the movie). Buzz exists as a three-dimensional action figure, a character in video games, television commercials, books, and even in his own animated (though not digital) movie as a 'real' space ranger.

To return to the text ('Source of Zurg's Power') at the source of Zurg's power, when in *Toy Story 2* Rex, the avid video-playing dinosaur, finds a book for sale at Al's Toy Barn telling how to defeat Zurg, it becomes *his* 'source of power.' Analogously, Disney imagines its own productions as the source of the cognitive development, and perhaps also of the purchasing power, of American toddlers. Preceding literacy, Disney products inform the youngsters' intellectual apparatus. Disney publishes with these, as with other movies, *A Disney First Reader*. In this Disney reader, *Howdy, Sheriff Woody!*, there is a 'Note to Parents' with instructions on teaching children to read, written by (or ascribed to) Patricia Koppman, past president of the International Reading Association. Before reading, before the spoken word, comes Disney: 'Talk with children before reading. Let them see how much they al-ready know about Disney characters. If they are unfamiliar with the movie basis of a book, take a few minutes to look at the cover and some of the illustrations to establish a context. Talking is important, since oral language precedes and supports reading.'[14] Yet the movie is alive to its own insufficiency as a 'basis,' which has connotations of material foundation or bottom; marketing (let alone scripting) begins well be-fore the movie has opened. Precedence is a concept that is radically compromised not only by the form and content of the movies but also by the fact that the *Toy Story* phenomenon does not clearly begin or end with the movies themselves. In short, like every other source of power, textuality (and in the world of these toys the idea that words and letters are *building blocks* is literalized and deconstructed) is a functional myth, both within the movies and for the numerous other products with which they are associated.

With movies made digitally, as Comay says, 'the sense of *interface* between mediums would radically change, from being a kind of limiting membrane between radically disparate modes of experience to being a complete porous or transparent switching station between essentially homogeneous or continuous modes.'[15] In combining such modes of experience, blending media, the digital movies extend this book's argument about the ghostly quality of seeing things. In the second chapter, I cited the opening monologue (actually unspoken thoughts inside the head of Stephen Dedalus) of the Proteus chapter of Joyce's *Ulysses:* 'Ineluctable modality of the visible: at least that if no more, thought through my eyes. Signatures of all things I am here to read.'[16] Trying to convince himself of the reality of things that appear to slip apperception like the tide, Stephen imagines cognition as an act of reading (at the same time as he is read by someone holding the book *Ulysses,* teasing Joyce's theme of metempsychosis). Invoking Bishop Berkeley, Shakespeare, and Plato, he also tries, ironically, to grasp a metaphysical reality or origin that eludes vision. Though it may seem a distant leap from Stephen to Buzz Lightyear, the comparison is instructive because it points to elements of Joyce's protean text that the digital medium picks up (the Homeric legend of Proteus from which Joyce draws also involves puppets endowed with life). Identifying with Hamlet, Stephen, like Joyce, contemplates potential sources of the self in language (philologically), in texts (hermeneutically), in family (genetically), in spirit (metaphysically), and in things (phenomenologically). These investigations centre on a problem of paternity epitomized by Hamlet's Ghost, which Stephen puts in Platonic terms, as he seeks the 'form of forms.' Buzz Lightyear's search for, or belief in, the form of forms, a source initially embedded in a video game, ends when he discovers that he is a toy. The discovery will prove emotionally liberating. The *Toy Story* movies celebrate an ongoing transformation in the nature and culture of visuality. They represent the liberal, democratic promise that has driven, and been driven by, the evolution of visual technologies since the nineteenth century and through modernism. These movies reflect on how the proliferation of images, copies, and simulacra may subvert hierarchical control. Cut loose from origins (such as Shakespeare's fathers, who claimed property in their children), these figures chart an increasingly fluid path between media and modes of experience.

*Toy Story,* as the Disney website grandiloquently proclaims, is the 'first completely computer-animated feature film in the history of motion pictures.'[17] That sense of the technology's newness, that kind of originality, is thematically crucial. *Toy Story* is 'a film unlike anything you've ever seen before,' we are told, 'with remarkably realistic animation of startling depth, dimension, and style.' Depth and dimension, however, are illusions. And, of course, it is not a *film* at all. In the first movie, when Andy's family moves, their house is sold by Virtual Realty. Moreover, the human characters who, like the toys, are composed entirely of pixels, occupy a reality far less vivid than the toys themselves, objects that continually and explicitly question their own reality. Lasseter chose toys as the protagonists in part because computer animation could do toys well; smooth plastic surfaces are ideal for computer animation. The animators made physical models of every character in the movie and scanned them into the computer using a 'kind of magnet.' Once the forms were on the computer, details, colour, clothing, and so on were added.[18] The animators employed maquettes, in short, not as material foundation but to test shapes and ideas. Retaining the idiom of depth, Pixar's technology creates a parable of decentred subjectivity that speaks to visual motifs that we have examined, from the 'gauds' of Shakespeare to the torn images of Beckett.

After Buzz loses his life to Zurg on the screen, we see that his battle has itself been an illusion (a video game) within an illusion (the movie). In Andy's room the 'camera' pans back, and we see that the game has been played by the plastic dinosaur Rex and watched by a spectator who is none other than Buzz himself. It is the first appearance in *Toy Story 2* of a trope that recurs in both movies, namely, the appearance of a character to himself in one of his commodified representations. The fact that our first glimpse of the 'real' Buzz in the second movie is in front of an image of himself on a television screen is a sign that his character has developed markedly from the first *Toy Story* to the second. Identity is not unitary or self-generated; it emerges not from thought (Descartes's *cogito*) but from a fictional situation. It must be imagined, with an emphasis on image, and, in this case, an image that is explicitly manufactured, reproduced, and marketed.

Thus, when the 'real' Buzz first appears in *Toy Story 2*, he is literally detached, amused by an image of himself that has been 'played by' another character. Buzz achieved self-consciousness in the first movie when he happened to see a commercial on television for the Buzz Lightyear action figures sold at Al's Toy Barn. (It reports that Buzz is not a flying toy, and he verifies this news when he falls from the top of a staircase.) He had been devastated to learn that he was not *the real* Buzz Lightyear but only a toy, a representation. Now Buzz has, in effect, accepted the limits of being limitless. 'Oh, you almost had him [Zurg],' says Buzz to the discouraged dinosaur: 'You're a better Buzz than I am.' The 'real Buzz' – for we see that previously we have been watching not *the* Buzz Lightyear but *a* Buzz Lightyear – comforts his friend with a line that signals one of the movies' key paradoxes: the need for self-knowledge which is knowledge that there is no core self. The real Buzz is not real.

When he finds himself in Al's Toy Barn, confronting an entire aisle of Buzz Lightyears, like a stroller in Benjamin's arcades, he seems overwhelmed by a kind of fantasy of resurrection. He walks down an enormous aisle awed by the appearance of an infinite number of boxes of replicas of himself, each of which promises to come to life. The first *Toy Story* movie had represented resurrection in terms that were mock-gothic; *Toy Story 2* naturalizes it. (*Toy Story 3* adopts an environmentalist motif: from garbage to recycling.) The instant replay of video game or television commercial or the mass assembly of the characters renders resurrection a commonplace. As the toys set out from the roof of Andy's house in quest of Woody, conflating Al's Toy Barn with infinity, Buzz utters his one variation on his famous slogan: 'To Al's Toy Barn,' he says, 'and beyond.' In Al's Toy Barn, Buzz confronts the image of his own potentially limitless repetition. Disney imagines infinite identical replicas of Buzz continuing after any individual Buzz is no more. (Recall that these movies emerged in the 1990s in the midst of ferocious debates about the ethics of cloning; in 1996 the aptly named sheep Dolly became the first mammal to be cloned from an adult somatic cell.)

In *Toy Story 2*, Woody, who knows that he is Andy's toy, has the key recognition scene. It is an almost classical moment of *anagnorisis*, when ignorance gives way to knowledge, creating a reversal. (For Woody as for Buzz, there is a crucial Oedipus complex; discovering his origins is an action fundamentally related to a struggle with and symbolic killing of a father figure.) Having been kidnapped, he is confronted by the other toys from the 'original' round-up gang. To his astonishment, he finds that they recognize him. 'Why, you don't know who you are!' says the Old Prospector, Stinky Pete, who literally lives in his *original* box and refers to Woody as 'the prodigal son.' One sympathizes with Woody's ignorance and wonder at the magnitude of what is to be revealed. 'You're valuable property!' exclaims Jesse, the cowgirl, as if that answers the question, and it does.

Woody's value is not use-value but rather a mystical quality that is a reflection of the social conditions in which the commodities find themselves and which dictate their relations to each other. Clearly, it is the rareness of (and nostalgia for) the 1950s nuclear family that these toys represent for their 1990s audience and especially the embattled position of the benevolent white patriarch that dictate Woody's own disproportionate exchange-value. While fathers appear in order to be overcome by both Buzz and Woody, Andy's father is entirely and inexplicably absent, not only from mundane activities but also from birthday parties, Christmas Eve, moving day, and taking Andy to sleep-away camp. The movies seem a fulfilment of the Oedipal dream in which Andy gets to live alone with his always available, non-professional mother, treating his infant sister with his own brand of benevolent paternalism. But the paternalism of Woody certainly carries over to the relationship between Woody and Andy, who treats his toy with a mixture of love and violence. The conclusion of *Toy Story 2* involves the acquiescence of Woody to his own mortality, which he relates fundamentally to the growing up of Andy. Woody, in short, is both a son and a father (spiritually). He stands in for, or is a kind of ghost of, Andy's absent father. But he does not realize the scope of his family relations until he is reunited with his 'original' gang. Jesse, Stinky Pete, and the toy horse Bull's Eye will enable Woody both to identify himself and to realize that identity is inseparable from the marketplace. The family too is a cultural product, artificial, projected by consumer desire, and ultimately (if there is an ultimate) not *really* there.

With great dramatic, indeed scopophilic, effect, Bull's Eye raises the dimmers so that Woody finds himself in the presence of what amounts to a shrine to himself. He is surrounded by images of his own face, on plates, lunch boxes, yo-yos. (He later explains to Buzz and his old pals, the toys that have come from Andy's collection to rescue him, 'I'm a yo-yo,' which causes snickers, as if seeing too many images of himself has made him crazy.) The culmination occurs when he backs into a giant billboard cut-out of himself. The moment is spooky and powerful, but it gives way instantly to Woody and the gang playing with images of him on all the paraphernalia, the gadgets that were spawned by the appeal of his image on a television program in 1957. Then they sit down to watch videos of the old show (*Woody's Round-Up*) on television. Although Woody will come to realize in a later reversal that 'what it's all about is to make some child happy,' he has irrevocably discovered who he *really* is, a spectral vision. And he begins to speak in the slogans that are printed on almost every image, slogans such as 'Hey Howdy Hey,' that we have not heard him use before. David Price tells an anecdote in which two of the Pixar producers happen upon a Burger King full of *Toy Story* products, where they realize that 'their' characters are now real things, not just ideas, and out in the world. The animators' reaction to *Toy Story* toys draws attention to the transformation of Woody, Buzz, et al. from real things (toys and maquettes), to representations of things, and back to real things again – but now changed because the representations engendered a change in meaning.[19]

Most important at this point in *Toy Story 2*, all the marketing that surrounded Woody's 1957 television show contributes substantially to both the form and the content of the rest of the movie. For instance, in the climactic scene, where Woody seeks to save Jesse and himself from a plane that is heading to Tokyo, he not only recalls but also *enacts* the never-aired final episode of his show from the 1950s. This performance will be 'Woody's Finest Hour!' He can only think of himself, even in his most dire moment, in terms of the cultural forms, and specifically the marketing campaign, that identify him. The heroic conclusion *is* Woody's finest hour, serving, in a haunting sense, as both an original *and* a resurrection.

Conventionally, a resurrection is a rising again, from the dead, from sleep, from a state of decay to an ideal form, a returning to life. For the toys Woody discovers in Al's apartment, staying in the box is directly figured as a form of death. The cowgirl Jesse struggles pitifully against being 'in storage' or 'in the dark.' Together they have patiently been awaiting their saviour.

Redemption may be defined, like resurrection, as a recovery, a restoration, or an act of liberation, but it is one that involves a payment or a ransom. The soul can be purchased at the expense of the body. In Christian poetry, for instance, the redemption of mankind through Christ's sacrifice is commonly figured in commercial terms. Redemption is purchased with the blood of Christ. I want to stress the commercial aspect of the term 'redemption'; the one who is redeemed is bought.[20] In the same sense, the resurrected becomes an object of consumption (Christ as Host). There is also a structural or temporal difference between resurrection and redemption. Resurrection implies a linear temporality through recurrence, history if not historicism. Redemption, by contrast, breaks or ends time. When Prince Hal says, in *Henry 4, Part 1* (1.2.217), that he plans on 'Redeeming time when men think least I will,' he doesn't just mean making up for lost time, but also imagines a kind of apotheosis of himself and his nation. Redemption suggests not historical but millennial time: To infinity and beyond.

*Toy Story 2* concentrates not only on resurrection, as the initial image of Buzz destroyed and then, surprisingly, whole suggests, but also on the theme of redemption. In *Toy Story 2* Woody is stolen from Andy's home by a new villain, not the sadistic next-door neighbour Sid but a fat capitalist, Al of Al's Toy Barn. The theft occurs after Woody himself has stolen out of the house to save another toy from being sold in a yard sale, an act of heroism first mistaken for suicide by the other toys, with whom we watch through a pair of toy binoculars.[21] The rescue mission goes awry when Woody has a *fall*, is thrown upon a table of junk for sale, and is discovered by the toy connoisseur.

The greedy Al fetishizes toys and lives not in the dreamy suburbs (Disney's pastoral ideal or world of 'Nature') but in the decadent city. However, Al is far from being a simple image of false consciousness. His aim, in fact, is to *remove* Woody from the consumer-driven economy. Woody completes a set of the 'original' round-up gang that Al has kept in storage, and he plans to cash in by selling the set to the Toy Museum in Japan. Clearly, the idea of completion or completeness is another aspect of redemption – making whole that which has been fragmented or broken (like *tikkun olam* in the Jewish mystical tradition). Al has a specific plan to redeem the toys, in completing the set, and it is Al who has Woody's arm repaired, giving Woody the sense that he is 'just like new.' Expressing his excitement when a toy-maker not only restores Woody's amputated arm but also repairs every knick or scratch, culminating in a smooth paint stroke that erases Andy's name from Woody's boot, Al exclaims, 'You're amazing! You're a genius! He's just like new!' The movie cuts immediately to a flashy marketing image; the word 'NEW!' on a bin of toys in Al's Toy Barn. Before the word stands Buzz Lightyear, perhaps not NEW himself, but about to confront avatars or new versions of himself (still in 'hyper-sleep'). The difference between being new and being *like* new is defined by self-consciousness. New toys do not know that they are new toys. The desire to be *like new*, always in conjunction with anxiety about decay or death, is the engine of the movie's plot, for it entails the recognition of artifice and the enabling of metaphor.

The key scene of the movie, therefore, is the one in which Woody is repaired. It represents the wonder of art as much as that of resurrection. Al has called in an old-fashioned artisan, a toy-maker like Geppetto, an ancient European immigrant who also embodies much of the post-war German-Jewish attitude about American cultural decadence. 'You can't rush art,' the old man tells Al, who asks how long he will take, as he is about to set to work. With his help, Al plans to remove the toys from historical time and potential breakage at the hands of child owners and to transfer them to the sphere of art – all for a price, of course.

In the historical life of a toy, the 'inevitable' is to end up in a yard sale. Woody's adventure began when he tried to rescue the hapless Wheezy, whose squeaker is broken. 'It's no use prolonging the inevitable,' Wheezy laments. 'We're all just one stitch away from here . . . to there [the yard sale, if not eternity].' Woody himself has ended up with Wheezy on a shelf, literally behind the 8-ball, and not taken to cowboy camp as he expected because his 'arm wrecked' when Andy was playing with him. On the shelf he has a vivid nightmare. He dreams that Andy comes home early from camp and immediately rushes up to play with him. Andy shakes Woody around the room in the familiar old way, chanting the William Tell Overture (the theme of the Lone Ranger, another figure of resurrection) until he catches a glimpse of the damaged arm and stops dead. 'Oh,' he says tonelessly, his eyes going dead like Woody's. 'You're broken. I don't want to play with you any more.' In an ironic reversal of Benjamin's theory of aura, it is a sign of death that the human owner does not return the object's gaze. He holds Woody out from his body and drops him, and Woody falls, through the floor and a scattered deck of cards (all aces of spades), through a narrow shaft of light in a surrounding pitch of darkness, and into a garbage can. Andy, looking down from far above, before closing what looks like a trap door on the darkness, says, his voice echoing in the distance, 'Bye, Woody.' Woody cries, 'No, Andy, NO!' as he struggles up out of the can, only to be pulled back by what we now see was already in the garbage, an animated snake of toy parts and amputated limbs, a muscular arm grabbing Woody around the neck and dragging him to darkness, at which point he wakes up.

Of course, no one really returns from the dead. Resurrection is a product of culture, a poetic and pictorial conceit. And Woody's dream draws explicitly on a tradition of purgatorial art.[22] His dream, like the video game with which the movie began, signifies the power of the imagination and again figures resurrection as the central phenomenon in the phantasmagoric life of toys. Reality is construed in symbols and, through the arrangement of symbols, in fiction. Freud has taught us that, in the dreams we experience when we sleep, we may discover our true selves, our deepest reality, but only because of the freedom of the *symbolic* imagination in that context. Woody's dream is especially important because when it begins he is not the only one who is unable to distinguish between dream and reality. The audience too experiences no shift from outside to inside Woody's wooden head, in contrast to the movie's one other dreamer, the all-too-human Al, who wakes up abruptly as Woody seeks to escape, crying out, 'No, officer, I swear!' But we learn no more since we do not share his interior life. In the case of Woody, there are no clear markers to signify the boundary between awake and dreaming, image and reflection. The dream begins for him and for us simultaneously. In retrospect, the pack of aces might have been a sign, but because the movie self-consciously and consistently manipulates questions about the status of reality in both form and content, there is literally and figuratively no solid ground on which to orient oneself. The movie itself does not capture a real image that is 'out there.' Woody and we may then recognize that he has had only a dream, but it intensifies his and our sense of the 'inevitable.'

It is precisely from such an inevitability that Al seeks (if for questionable motives) to remove Woody, turning him, in effect, into an icon and a work of art. Al does not adhere to the bland conformity of the suburban world of minivans and freshly cut lawns (his lawn is painted on the side of a building). He represents an important relationship between redemption and representation. Like Sid, Al forces the toys into a liminal space, a space of self-reflection where unpleasant aspects of ideology become clear. Recognizing the ethos that props this world up, he does not hesitate to say: 'Everything's for sale ... or trade.' Al's Toy Barn itself is a self-conscious reflection of the yard sale at Andy's house. The Toy Barn represents an image of the bucolic paradise, the extraordinary plenty, and the innocence of nature that characterize America, but the rural scene is a mural painted on a brick wall of a commercial building. The Toy Barn is in a city on an extremely dangerous highway filled with traffic (a revision of the yellow brick road). Wherever one seeks Nature, the uncorrupted or the pure, culture is already there, whether the faux agri-*culture* of Al's Toy Barn or the popular culture of Walt Disney.

Furthermore, the child in the movies is hardly pure, likable though he may be. Central to this drama of redemption is the fact that the Christ-figure Woody (note especially the images of Woody on the cross in Al's apartment) is damaged *by Andy*. Early in each movie, Andy plays with his toys in a self-contained action of his own imagining and making; in short, he stages a drama and, in doing so, as in any play-within-a-play, comments meaningfully, if unintentionally, on the poetics of the larger work. The first movie begins with a bank robbery. The villain is

One-Eyed Bart (aka Mr Potato Head), but the voice is Andy's. When Bart gloats over his stash, kissing the coins spilled on the floor and chuckling, 'Money, money, money,' he speaks with *Andy's* voice and enacts the drama that *Andy* imagined. That line will return, when Al happily gloats, 'Money, baby,' or clucks, 'Buck, buck, bucks,' over his stolen toys in the sequel, effectively connecting the evil toy-store owner with the good boy. Taking pictures of his complete set to send to Mr Konishi at the museum in Japan, Al laughs, 'It's like printing my own money.' Toys represent money, and money represents toys.

The play with which Andy begins *Toy Story 2* is a hostage taking. Bo Peep has been kidnapped by Evil Dr Pork-Chop (significantly the piggy bank) and must be ransomed or redeemed by Woody. Toys can not only be redeemed but also imagined only in terms of money. (The first image we see is a wanted poster featuring Mr Potato Head as an outlaw with a price on his head.) When Andy ventriloquizes for the toys, it is crucial to recognize that the voice that gives utterance to 'evil,' even in play, is ultimately the same as that which gives voice to 'good': good and evil are not only imagined but also dramatized by the same organizing consciousness. Woody, of course, refuses the options offered by the pig and, with the help of his pal Buzz Lightyear, restores Bo Peep to freedom. But Woody does 'pay' for this victory over evil, for in the final moment of the game, with his arm hooked in that of Buzz, a seam pops. Woody is damaged not by an enemy but by a friend, by Andy himself. It is Andy, not his mother, who will decide to leave Woody at home, instead of taking him to cowboy camp. When Andy's Mom puts Woody on a shelf, she utters one of the movie's key lines, 'Toys don't last forever.' The words hang in the air as the human characters leave the screen.

Yet the phenomenon of cultural recycling and reproduction both within and surrounding these movies contradicts the sense of limitation to which the line gives voice. 'As Andy's favorite toy,' the Disney website reports, 'Woody has starred in such Andy productions as "Showdown at the Kiddy Corral," "High Noon Nap," and "Station Wagons Ho!" Named provocatively for Woody Strode, an African-American actor who had important roles in several John Ford movies in addition to playing slaves, a rebellious gladiator in *Spartacus,* and the title role of *Black Jesus,* Woody has mastered such legendary western phrases as "There's a snake in my boots!" and "Somebody poisoned the water hole!"'[23] Woody's partial origin in John Ford films, the importance of his role as an actor in 'Andy productions,' his own limited rhetorical range, signified by a string that activates his voice box, and the 'legendary western phrases' that he has 'mastered' all indicate the degree to which he is ideologically inscripted. All the toys are literally inscribed with Andy's name on the soles of their feet; that is the source of their identity, as we see when the 'real' Buzz distinguishes himself from the Buzz who tackled him in the toy store. It does not seem unreasonable to wonder, in this movie that self-consciously employs anagrams or 'jumbles of let-ters' that indicate ownership (Al's licence plate is LZTBRN for Al's Toy Barn), if *Andy's*, the name on the boot of the 'real' Woody doll, might be a clever inscription and near anagram of *Disney*, particularly given tensions arising from Disney's ownership of Pixar productions. Woody may be 'an original,' with a hand-painted face and hand-stitched poly-vinyl hat, but the essence of Woody is a collection of canned phrases and gestures, codes that only *signify* originality. He is a cultural artefact. Woody's 'finest hour' (a marketing slogan from his days as a famous puppet on television) will be the resurrection of a used cowboy-doll.

Resurrection implies a set of boundaries by which to distinguish the return from the original. It is precisely that assumption that is chal-lenged in *Toy Story* and *Toy Story 2*, itself a return. The intelligent toys in both movies are obsessed with their own identities – principally, with the problem of having no discernable origin – and, if the market-ing people at Disney play their cards right, no foreseeable end. When Buzz Lightyear is introduced in *Toy Story*, the rest of the toys in the room gather around him, awed by his colourful and noisy gadgets. Significantly, the first question they ask is, 'Where are you from?' They expect him to answer, 'China' or 'Singapore,' where most American toys are manufactured, or else 'Hasbro' or 'Mattel,' the name of a company that makes toys. But Buzz is still deluded about origins. He explains that he is from the gamma quadrant of the galaxy and proceeds to utter, verbatim, the fiction printed on the back of his box. The motto not only of Buzz but also of the *Toy Story* movies is 'To infinity and beyond!' And I believe that part of the appeal of that line for children is that it cap-tures some of their own confusion about origins and their own sense of limitlessness. For closely related to that sense of boundlessness is, as we have seen in the opening sequence of the second movie, the game of searching for a source (Zurg's power) that does not exist or is, at best, illusory. We become aware of a circular logic. Buzz's beginning (and the movie's) is in an ending ('Game Over': death of the simulacrum of Buzz). Like the character Jack/Ernest in Oscar Wilde's *Importance of*

*Being Earnest,* whose beginning was in a 'terminus' when, as a baby, he was mistakenly swapped for a three-volume novel, Buzz and Woody are forced to recognize the art that constructs their identities. They are never present but always represented. Like ghosts, their beginning is their end and vice versa.

Today the mechanical reproduction of a work of art is nothing new, to put it mildly. In media that seem increasingly old-fashioned, from the printing press to film, mechanical reproduction maintains, even if in a barely minimal form, an indexical relation to the original. The quality of film as index, as opposed to icon, depends on its being an imprint of light, a trace left by a real body. That is, it has a direct relation with its subject, as, to paraphrase film scholar Gilberto Perez, a footprint has with a foot. Perez distinguishes between icon and index by suggesting that 'as icon the photograph was invented by painters; as index, by chemists.'[24] I have purposely avoided using the term 'film' to discuss *Toy Story* because, starting a development that has taken over the field of animation, the movies were not shot with film. Entirely computer generated, they cannot have even the faintest trace of an original unless audience members project one fantastically. There is no space between the original and the beholder since there is no original. And, if there is no original, what can authenticity mean? What is demanded of us is a new mode of perception. The toys are aware, or become aware, of the fact that their lives cannot be measured in individual terms but only in those of mass production. 'You Are a Toy!' is the line shouted at any object that thinks itself special (a 'real' space ranger or cowboy, for example). To be a toy in a Disney movie is to be reproduced.

The movie invites viewers to sympathize and identify with Woody and Buzz on a personal level, but only as they are also to be identified on a historical and cultural level. They are not only represented but also representative. They are and can only be American, and this aspect also informs the way in which the personal, the mythic, and the historical are conjoined in their characters. In the end, Woody's personal redemption will, by extension, figure a kind of historical redemption, the redeeming of a particular vision of an ideal America. The rhetorical forms that represent both historical movement and the timeless journey of the soul are shown to be malleable; these narratives are not actually in opposition but are mutually sustaining. 'One of the most powerful unifying elements of the culture,' as Sacvan Bercovitch writes in *The Puritan Origins of the American Self,* is 'the persistence of the redemptive meaning of America.'[25] Disney celebrates the representative self as American and the American self as the embodiment of a prophetic universal design, inverting secular values in the mould of quasi-sacred teleology. But the very idea of origins becomes radically ironic because the sentimental spirit of toys is the spirit of capitalism.

Far from positing a theological source or end, a *telos*, these movies represent infinity above all as a marketing phenomenon, which assumes that children can take a moral pleasure in property and discovers an educative value in the capitalist free market. *Infinity* is a word that can be read if printed or heard if uttered and even an image – of outer space – that can be visualized metonymically. But Disney presses the viewer to imagine a space and time before and beyond the letter, word, or image. Before the letter, as the *Disney Reader* tells us, is Disney, which signifies a way of thinking and an attitude towards history. Like Buzz dropping through a giant Z, the viewer is presented with signs of forbiddenness and then ushered into those spaces to discover only the values that structure normative experience spelled large. If, as Georg Lukács argues, 'the problem of commodities ... [is] the central, structural problem of capitalist society in all its aspects,' Woody's adventure shows how far commodity exchange has influenced the '*total* outer and inner life of society.'[26] But how do we judge that influence? Woody is the representative American, and his personal redemption will, by extension, figure a kind of historical redemption, the redeeming of a particular vision of an always inauthentic, and ever-youthful (not necessarily puerile) America. Woody's identity, his very name, is inseparable from the material with which he is made; form is content and vice versa. Inside is outside.

The fantasy of resurrection that *Toy Story* and *Toy Story 2* depict is a fantasy of unlimited commodification and redemption (i.e., profit). This theme persists, though it is complicated, in *Toy Story 3*, but that is a story for another book. To return to the quotation from Baudelaire with which this chapter began, these movies both exemplify and subvert the metaphysical life of toys. Neither Sid nor Al nor Andy is interested in the spirit of toys. For good guys and bad guys, toys, for better or worse, are commodities. Those characters, Andy, Sid, and Al, as the frequency of point-of-view shots suggest, are surrogates for the audience. The toys may come alive for the extradiegetic viewer's pleasure, but that life only serves to dramatize the toys' and, indeed, the viewers' own commodification. If we seek metaphysics, we only experience our own, perhaps subconscious, awareness of the movies' intertextual embeddedness (the textuality of our own minds). What is before or beyond or behind the letter? There is nothing outside of culture. As the young Samuel Beckett wrote in *Proust*, 'It is possible (for those who take an interest in such speculations) to consider the resurrection of the soul as a final piece of insolence from the same source. It insists on that most necessary, wholesome and monotonous plagiarism – the plagiarism of oneself.'[27] The 'source' to which Beckett refers is memory, a reference that is meant to be ironic. But to recognize that one continuously (infinitely) plagiarizes oneself and is never original need not be a source of modernist despair. On the contrary, it can suggest a fruitful, that is, liberal, pattern of creative destruction.

Pixar's explorations of things in movies since the first *Toy Story*, from *Wall-E* to *Up*, are also aetiologies of selves, whether of toys, robots, or old men. Sentimental as these movies tend to be about interpersonal (or interthing) relations, they do not sentimentalize the idea of a soul or human essence. On the contrary, like recent entertainments in what Matthew Smith calls 'VR cyberspace,' or multimedia-generated virtual space that absorbs spectators in computer-generated 'experiences,' the dreams of Pixar's things turn out to be extremely ironic. As Smith says of other cyber-arts, the realization of these movies, or the characters' discovery of their own reality, 'occurs within and by means of a center-less space devoid of essential content.'[28] That is what I take to be the meaning of the endless loop of the show-tune 'Put on Your Sunday Clothes,' from *Hello, Dolly*, that plays in Wall-E's trash-compactor middle; or, in Pixar's first venture into 3D, *Up*, the importance of the massive cluster of balloons. Surprisingly for Pixar, *Up* does not overtly exploit the thematic possibilities of the new visual technology, with figures leaping out towards the viewer, until one reflects on the movie's central trope, the thousands of large, round, colourful, and empty balloons. The O at the source of power, or emptiness at the centre of the real, to paraphrase Lacan, is not a subject of regret or mourning. Far from it, the emptiness at the centre of the real, as the balloons show, is the condition of all that is uplifting in these movies.

Pixar's extraordinarily sophisticated thematic as well as technological investment in the three-dimensional reality of its toys is a key feature of *Toy Story 3*, which also appears in Disney Digital 3D. This third movie richly plays on the 3D fad. Like the first two movies, *Toy Story 3* incorporates multiple media in a way that is both simply 'realistic' and meta-cinematically lays bare the device. The movie, in which Andy leaves for college, presents expository material – another aetiology of self and technology – in a flashback via a fictional handheld digital camera. Using the video setting, Andy's Mom captures him (and herself trying to figure the technology out) in the viewfinder, as we watch with her from her point of view. This use of an internal camera might seem a reiteration of a classic reflection on the partiality of viewing things, as in Renoir's *Boudu Saved from Drowning*, when, through the lens of a telescope employed by a character in the movie, the spectator sees Boudu walking and then attempting suicide. But Pixar's use of the camera does more than imply an analogy between our viewing and that of a character in the movie. It comments on the visual mechanics of the mediating technology itself.

Older methods of stereoscopy, or 3D filming, employed two cameras and superimposed the images (a pair of 2D images) on the two-dimensional screen. Filters on the 3D glasses allowed one image to enter each eye, and the human brain did the rest, reconstructing the three-dimensional image. Instead of using two real cameras, Digital 3D technology creates a second digital 'camera' as a computer program within a computer program. Unlike standard animation, which uses drawings that create the illusion of perspective (the invisible side of a character in profile is assumed by the spectator but does not really exist), the invisible dimensions of digital characters and objects, whether in movies or computer games, actually exist – in the sense that they exist at all – in virtual reality, as indicated by movements of the computer's internal 'camera.' So, these digital 3D characters have more dimensions, are more thing-like, than Bugs Bunny or Betty Boop. This technology, like the superimpositions in American spirit photography of the 1860s, gives new meaning to the notion of plagiarism of oneself.

Combining a vision of spiritual death and a yearning for rebirth, Symbolism, and Puritanism, in *The Waste Land*, T.S. Eliot paints an infernal and phantasmagorical picture that speaks with peculiar appropriateness to Pixar's richly metaphorical boxes of old toys. In the poem Eliot asks what grows out of modernity's heap of rubbish:

> ... Son of man,
> You cannot say, or guess, for you know only
> A heap of broken images, where the sun beats ...

Pixar's artists and technicians and their imagined toys would not disagree. From the robot Wall-E, a pathetic, rolling emblem of broken images, designed to clean up a trash-covered planet, to the broken, junked, and recycled characters of the *Toy Story* movies, Pixar indicates that broken images in both 'real' and cyberspace pile up in a continuum that transcends any notion of a fundamental separation of the digital from earlier media and models of time and space. Neither would Pixar's employees find this insight – that we are only a heap of broken images – a cause for despair. On the contrary, in Pixar's movies the recognition that the self is a heap of broken images is a condition of resurrection and renewal and, if that be to the profit of someone, all the better. In the new 'Toy Story Mania!' attraction at Disney World, consumers can don 3D glasses, climb aboard carnival-themed tram vehicles, and enter the animated world of Woody, Buzz, Jessie, Rex, and Hamm, not only seeing things, but also, in an added '4D' dimension, feeling virtual objects whoosh by. In form and content, Pixar films and spin-offs epitomize the liberal culture that consumes them. Four hundred years removed from Descartes, images upon images are what we have become and all that we can hope to be.

# Notes

## Introduction

1 Zemeckis, 'Behind the Scenes.'
2 See Castle, 'Phantasmagoria,' 132.
3 Dickens, *A Christmas Carol*, 43.
4 Zemeckis, 'Behind the Scenes.'
5 Dickens, *A Christmas Carol*, 89–90.
6 Ibid., 76, 71.
7 Ibid., 70.
8 Ibid., 99, 102.
9 Derrida, *Specters of Marx*, 7, emphasis in original.
10 'Toute la vie des sociétés dans lesquelles règnent les conditions modernes de production s'annonce comme une immense accumulation de *spectacles*.' Debord, *La société du spectacle*, 9; emphasis in original. Unless otherwise specified, all translations are the author's.
11 Arnheim, *Visual Thinking*, 294.
12 Homer, *The Odyssey*, book 19 ('Penelope and Her Guest'), 403.
13 Ibid., 405.
14 Brooks, *Realist Vision*, 6.
15 This tradition depends in part on etymologies of the name Homer. See Chantraine, *Dictionnaire étymologique*, vol. 2 (3–4): 797 ad loc. and Liddell and Scott, *A Greek-English Lexicon*. Also, Graziosi, *Inventing Homer*, 133.
16 Arnheim, *Visual Thinking*, 105.
17 Quotations of Shakespeare are from *The Riverside Shakespeare*.
18 In his essay 'The Uncanny,' Freud writes, 'I think, that the feeling of something uncanny is directly attached to the figure of the Sand-Man, that is, to the idea of being robbed of one's eyes'; http://www-rohan.sdsu

.edu/~amtower/uncanny.html. In this comment about uncanny insight, I also paraphrase Stanley Cavell's critique of philosophy in *Must We Mean What We Say?* 1.

19 Chaudhuri, *Staging Place*, 198.

20 Ibsen, *Et Dukkehjem*, 7.

21 Ibid., 151.

22 Locke, *Essay Concerning Human Understanding*, 1: 96; also see Sorensen, *Seeing Dark Things*, 4.

23 Brooks, *Realist Vision*, 2.

24 A discussion of where 'human truth' exists in performance runs through decades of writing in theatre studies. For instance, Richard Schechner writes in 1973: 'The great argument of modern theater between the naturalist and the theatricalist boils down to this: *Where does human truth lie? On the surface, in the behavior men show everyday, or in the depths, behind social masks?* The naturalists strive for a replication of just those everyday details that represent the essential man. The theatricalist strives for means to penetrate or surpass the masks of daily life in order to reveal the essential man' (original italics). Schechner, *Environmental Theater*, 126. More recently, for reference to the 'magic' of theatrical performance, see Dolan, *Utopia in Performance*, 4, 17.

25 Sofer, *The Stage Life of Props*, vi, 6, 17, 60.

26 Brown, 'Thing Theory,' 1–22, and *A Sense of Things*, 4–5, 17.

27 Brown, 'How to Do Things with Things (A Toy Story),' 935–64; http://www.jstor.org/stable/1344113.

28 Shakespeare, *A Midsummer Night's Dream*, 1.1.32; 5.1.5, 17. *Riverside Shakespeare*, 217–49. Among the many excellent works on early modern material culture and material things in Shakespeare in particular, see Jones and Stallybrass, *Renaissance Clothing and the Materials of Memory*.

29 I here thank my research assistant, Sarah Kriger, and animator Judith Kriger for explaining the technologies of animation to me.

30 Stewart quoted in Baird, 'Screen Savers,' M3.

31 Levin, 'Introduction,' *Modernity and the Hegemony of Vision*, 2.

32 Johnson, *Persons and Things*, 3.

33 Foucault, *The Order of Things*, xiv; Kant, *Critique of Pure Reason*, trans. Werner S. Pluhar, 23–5 (B xviii–xxii).

34 Louis Kaplan, *The Strange Case of William Mumler, Spirit Photographer*, 1–34.

35 The image and caption are reproduced in Kaplan (plate 1). Note: The caption, presumably Mumler's, reads, 'Mary Todd Lincoln with the Spirit of Her Husband President Abraham Lincoln and Son Thaddeus.' Lincoln's son, however, was named Thomas 'Tad' Lincoln, not Thaddeus.

36  Kant, *Critique of Judgment*, trans. Werner S. Pluhar, 196 (327).
37  See Mitchell's discussion of *ekphrasis*, the verbal representation of visual representation, in *Picture Theory*, 152.
38  I am grateful to Sarah Krieger for her insights on this subject.
39  Scarry, *Resisting Representation*, 50–1.
40  Shakespeare, *Midsummer Night's Dream*, 5.1.24–6.
41  See Jackson, *Professing Performance*, 3, 40–78.
42  See de Bolla, 'The Visibility of Visuality,' 68.
43  Merleau-Ponty, 'Eye and Mind,' 169. Also see Judovitz, 'Vision, Representation, and Technology in Descartes,' 63.
44  Shakespeare, *Midsummer Night's Dream*, 1.1.56.
45  Jackson, *Professing Performance*, 13, 63.
46  Fried, *Art and Objecthood*, 148–68.
47  Baudelaire, 'Morale du joujou,' 201–7; 'A Philosophy of Toys.'
48  See Ackerman, 'The Prompter's Box: Back to the Future,' 225–34.

## Chapter 1:  A Spirit of Giving in *A Midsummer Night's Dream*

1  Ficino, *Commentary on Plato's* Symposium, 125.
2  Smith, *Theory of Moral Sentiments*, 8.
3  Ibid., 3.
4  Wilde, 'The Portrait of Mr. W. H.,' 324–5. All quotations of Wilde are from *Complete Works of Oscar Wilde*.
5  Plato, *Symposium*, 48 (188b). Citations from Plato are taken from an updated version of Benjamin Jowett's well-known translation, entitled *The Symposium of Plato*. The more recent edition of Jowett's translation slightly revises the language of Jowett's Oxford edition, and it lacks the Stephanus pagination of the earlier edition. This chapter cites page numbers from the 1983 edition plus the Stephanus pagination found in the Oxford (1953) edition and many other modern translations of Plato.
6  Nussbaum, *Love's Knowledge*, 114.
7  Ibid., original emphasis.
8  Weiner, *Inalienable Possessions*, 2.
9  Marx, *Capital*, 163.
10  Ibid., 166.
11  Mauss, *The Gift*, 22.
12  Montrose, '"Shaping Fantasies,"' 56.
13  See Hayman, *Brecht*, 219.
14  Greenblatt, *Marvelous Possessions*, 71, original emphasis.
15  Ibid., 77, original emphasis.

16  Montaigne, 'On Cannibals,' 109, 114, 117.
17  Montrose, 'Shaping Fantasies,' 41.
18  Greenblatt, *Marvelous Possessions*, 71.
19  While a princess of the Amazons may have resided near the Black Sea for the Greeks, for Elizabethans, at least by 1596, when *A Midsummer Night's Dream* was first performed and Walter Raleigh published his creative travelogue *Discovery of Guiana*, the Amazon would have been understood to have referred to the New World of South America, just as the wood outside of Athens was also very much an English space. Montaigne makes this connection between ancient conquest of the 'new world' surrounding the Black Sea and sixteenth-century imperialism across the Atlantic in his 1580 *Essays* (105–7). The habit of thought that Montaigne, Raleigh, and others exhibit collapses the New World into the classical past.
20  Plato, *Symposium*, 64 (200a).
21  Ibid., 68 (202e), emphasis added.
22  Ficino, *Commentary on Plato's* Symposium, 109.
23  Weiner, *Inalienable Possessions*, 15.
24  Jones and Stallybrass, *Renaissance Clothing*, 263.
25  Plato, *Symposium*, 82 (213b–c).
26  Ibid., 78 (210b).
27  Jowett, Introduction to Plato's *Symposium*, 20.
28  Leggatt, *Shakespeare's Comedy of Love*, 113–14.
29  'Unde qui docet, minister est potius quàm magister. Quapropter Socrates apud Platonem in libro de scientia Theęteto inquit se filium obstretricis esse, & obstetrici persimilem: utpote qui in erudiendis hominibus non inducat scientiam, sed educat, sicut obstetricĭ conceptos iam foetus educunt' (*Theologica Platonica* 14: 180).

## Chapter 2: Visualizing Hamlet's Ghost

1  G.W.F. Hegel, *The Phenomenology of Mind*, 75. Several influential critical studies situate the origins of Modernist literature in Romanticism; they include Wilson, *Axel's Castle*, Kermode, *Romantic Image*, and Frank, *The Widening Gyre*. Each of these works, however, makes totalizing claims about form and pays little attention to historicity. For a critique of this literary critical tradition, see Riquelme, *Harmony of Dissonances*. Further, it should be noted that other studies of the modern drama situate its origins in aspects of Romanticism. Benjamin Bennett claims that in the *Phenomenology* Hegel lays the groundwork for a theory of drama; *Modern Drama and German Classicism*, 255–6. Robert Brustein's *Theatre of Revolt*

describes a thematic continuity between the modern drama and 'the second wave of Romanticism ... the dark fury of Nietzsche with his radical demands for a total transformation of man's spiritual life' (8). And monographs on individual authors, such as those on Ibsen by Durbach, *Ibsen the Romantic*, and Johnston, *The Ibsen Cycle,* trace the influence of Romantic thinkers on modern playwrights. Martin Scofield investigates the importance of the 'image' of Hamlet in 'modern' literature generally in *The Ghosts of Hamlet.*

2  Taylor, *Sources of the Self,* 157.
3  Descartes, *Meditations,* 3: 167.
4  Taylor, *Hegel and Modern Society,* 10.
5  Löwith, *From Hegel to Nietzsche,* 6.
6  Dowden, *Shakespeare,* 133.
7  Hillman, 'Visceral Knowledge,' 81–106.
8  Freud, *The Interpretation of Dreams,* 366–7. Also see Lyotard, *Discours, figure,* 163–89.
9  Lacan, *The Four Fundamental Concepts of Psycho-Analysis,* 35.
10  Trilling, *Sincerity and Authenticity,* 5.
11  Some more recent psychoanalytic readings of *Hamlet* have focussed on the trope of writing. See Garber, *Shakespeare's Ghost Writers,* 137–49, and Sibony, '*Hamlet:* A Writing-Effect.' Herman Melville compares reading the landscape of Hawthorne's soul to reading that of Shakespeare in 'Hawthorne and His Mosses.'
12  In *Realms of the Self,* Arthur Ganz argues that an 'emphasis on the dissociation of the interior and exterior worlds reminds us that Pirandello's dramatic roots extend back through the romantics to Shakespeare, most particularly to Hamlet' (189). Erich Heller describes Hamlet as a 'prince of the mind' for whom nothing 'could possibly be in perfect accord with his inner being'; *The Artist's Journey into the Interior and Other Essays,* 145. Northrop Frye remarks: 'During the nineteenth century, and through much of the twentieth, *Hamlet* was regarded as Shakespeare's central and most significant play, because it dramatized a central preoccupation of the age of Romanticism: the conflict of consciousness and action.' See *Northrop Frye on Shakespeare,* 99.
13  Eliot, '*Hamlet,*' 45.
14  Shattuck, *The Hamlet of Edwin Booth,* 115, 117. Shattuck's book is my primary source for information on Booth's *Hamlet.* Shattuck has published Charles Clarke's record of the 1870 production along with the history of Booth's *Hamlet,* photographs, and citations from contemporary critics. All further references to Booth's *Hamlet* are taken from this work.

15  Jonathan Crary details a set of technological innovations such as the invention of the stereoscope, by which, beginning in the 1820s, vision became
'inseparable from transience – that is, from new temporalities, speeds, experiences of flux and obsolescence, a new density and sedimentation of the
structure of visual memory.' *Techniques of the Observer*, 20–1.

16  Goethe, *Theory of Colours*, 1.

17  Shattuck, *The Hamlet of Edwin Booth*, 131–2.

18  Booth's Hamlet 'never forgot ... that he was vastly different from practical,
realistic men of the nineteenth century.' After his first vision of the Ghost,
he is left 'in a state of high excitement. His wonder and fear were fresh
upon him' (159). Horatio, by contrast, is described by J. Dover Wilson as
a disciple of the sixteenth-century thinker Reginald Scot, whose view was
'frankly and entirely sceptical ... What he contests is the possibility of
spirits assuming material form'; Wilson, 'Introduction,' in *Lewes Lavater: Of
Ghosts and Spirites Walking by Nyght*, xvii.

19  Stanley Cavell suggests that 'our eagerness [like Hamlet's] to believe the
Ghost is fortified by a ... concern over the potentially foul condition of our
own imaginations'; 'Hamlet's Burden of Proof,' 183. Hamlet exemplifies
the notion that to exist 'the human being has the burden of proving that
he or she exists, and that this burden is discharged in thinking your existence.' Cavell suggests that the epitome of this idea is Descartes's *cogito*: 'To
exist is to take your existence upon you, to enact it, as if the basis of human
existence is theater, even melodrama. To refuse this burden is to condemn
yourself to skepticism ... Hamlet's extreme sense of theater I take as his
ceaseless perception of theater, say show, as an inescapable or metaphysical mark of the human condition'; ibid., 187.

20  Coleridge, *Lectures 1808–1819 on Literature*, 5.1: 386.

21  Cited in Ellmann, *Oscar Wilde*, 251.

22  Abrams, *Natural Supernaturalism*, 12–13.

23  Coleridge mentions the 'Terra incognita of the Human Mind' in notes for
his Shakespeare lectures. See *Lectures 1808–1819*, 5.2: 287.

24  Carlyle, *Sartor Resartus*, 1: 192.

25  Brooks, *The Melodramatic Imagination*, 16.

26  Strindberg, *Inferno and From an Occult Diary*, 147.

27  Crary, *Techniques of the Observer*, 9.

28  Ibid., 14.

29  The camera obscura was a particularly apt metaphor for subjectivity. As
Crary explains, it 'performs an operation of individuation; that is, it necessarily defines an observer as isolated, enclosed, and autonomous within
its dark confines. It impels a ... withdrawal from the world, in order to

regulate and purify one's relation to the manifold contents of the now "exterior" world. Thus the camera obscura is inseparable from a certain metaphysic of interiority: it is a figure for both the observer who is nominally a free sovereign individual and a privatized subject . . . cut off from a public exterior world' (ibid., 40).

30  *Lectures upon Shakespeare*, 4: 145.

31  Wordsworth, *The Poetical Works of William Wordsworth*, 5: 313–39; 'Prospectus,' 1.1576–7.

32  Schopenhauer, *The World as Will and Representation*, 2: 27. As the oldest blind man says in Maeterlinck's *Les aveugles*, 'Les yeux en savent plus que les mains' ('Eyes know more than hands') (107).

33  Schopenhauer, *The World as Will and Representation*, 2: 22.

34  In his 1818 lecture on *The Tempest*, Coleridge articulates a notion of inner and, hence, 'spiritual' vision. His idea is strikingly idiosyncratic, yet it is important for indicating at least a confusion both about the site of phenomenal experience and about the competing claims of the spiritual and the material. Coleridge remarks that 'the principal and only genuine excitement ought to come from within, – from the moved and sympathetic imagination; whereas, where so much is addressed to the more external senses of seeing and hearing, the spiritual vision is apt to languish, and the attraction from without will withdraw the mind from the proper and only legitimate interest which is intended to spring from within' (*Collected Works*, 5.1: 268–9). Significantly, the senses of seeing and hearing are *relatively* external.

35  Schopenhauer, *The World as Will and Representation*, 2: 22; emphasis added.

36  Ruskin, *The Art Criticism of John Ruskin*, 23–4.

37  Quoted in Shattuck, *The Hamlet of Edwin Booth*, 51. A correspondent for the *Evening Post* writes of Booth's production: 'Every art has, of course, been used to make the apparition as unsubstantial as possible' (ibid., 119).

38  Berkeley, *A New Theory of Vision*, 33.

39  These notes are taken from lecture 3 of the 1813 series in *Lectures 1808–1819 on Literature*, 1: 540.

40  Goethe, *Wilhelm Meister's Apprenticeship*, 105.

41  Goethe, *Theory of Colour*, 16, 21.

42  Crary, *Techniques of the Observer*, 68.

43  Goethe, *Theory of Colour*, 10.

44  Goethe, *Wilhelm Meister's Apprenticeship*, 198.

45  William Charles Macready notes in his journal that he was asked to 'speak' the closet scene alone at Rugby. Macready, the great English Shakespearean actor of his day, comments that during the spring of 1841,

while playing Hamlet nearly every night, he is also reading *Wilhelm Meister*. Macready, *The Journal of William Charles Macready*, 36, 152.

46 *Charles Lamb on Shakespeare*, 29, 18.

47 Many explanations for Gertrude's singular blindness to the Ghost have been hazarded over the years. Among the most prominent, A.C. Bradley argues unconvincingly in *Shakespearean Tragedy* that 'a ghost, in Shakespeare's day, was able for any sufficient reason to confine its manifestation to a single person in company' (139–40). Harley Granville-Barker says easily that Gertrude is just 'spiritually blind'; see *Prefaces to Shakespeare*, 3: 116. J. Dover Wilson suggests that 'Gertrude is unable to see the "gracious figure" because her eyes are held by the adultery she has committed,' and now she is cut off from her dead husband; see *What Happens in* Hamlet, 254–5.

48 Castle, 'Phantasmagoria,' 36.

49 Crary, *Techniques of the Observer*, 127.

50 Goethe, *Sorrows of Young Werther*, 84.

51 Castle, 'Phantasmagoria,' 29.

52 Dickens, *Great Expectations*, 279.

53 Castle, 'Phantasmagoria,' 29.

54 Crary, *Techniques of the Observer*, 24.

55 Strindberg, 'A Glance into Space,' 165.

56 See Kern, *Culture of Time and Space*, 143.

57 Strindberg, *Ghost Sonata*, 190–1.

58 William Archer's influential translation is the source of the English title. But the Norwegian *Gengangere* emphasizes recurrence and motion: 'It means literally "Again-goers," spirits that "walk,"' according to Archer's prefatory note to *Ibsen's Prose Dramas*, n.p. Yet, 'ghost' and 'gengangere' have similar connotations. See *William Archer on Ibsen*, 107–12.

59 In quoting from Ibsen, I follow Rolf Fjelde's translation, the best to date, of Ibsen in *The Complete Major Prose Plays*.

60 See Fergusson, *The Idea of Theater*. Fergusson writes: 'What Mrs Alving sees changes in the course of the play, just as what Oedipus sees changes as one veil after another is removed from the past and the present. The underlying form of *Ghosts* is that of the tragic rhythm as one finds it in *Oedipus Rex*' (151).

61 In a review of the American Repertory Theatre production for the Boston *Phoenix*, Carolyn Clay remarks, 'In Robert Brustein's production of *Ghosts*, the title characters are things that go bump in the light ... In the end, as young Oswald suffers his sudden, debilitating syphilitic attack, there is an eerie, piercing sound; all the doors fly open, as if at some supernatural

instigation; and the sun also rises.' Brustein is quoted in the review as insisting that there are actual ghosts in the play, the setting is a 'haunted house.' The production indicates the difficulty of realizing such an idea dramaturgically while maintaining the integrity of Ibsen's realist text.

62  Szondi, *Theory of the Modern Drama,* 16.

63  Ibid., 7, emphasis added.

64  Bergson, 'Laughter,' 70. Goethe commonly refers to 'inner form,' as opposed to rigid, external forms. For more recent challenges to a mimetic model of representation, see Gadamer's discussion of 'play' in *Truth and Method,* 109; and Iser on the 'floating signifier' in *The Fictive and the Imaginary,* 31.

65  Bergson, 'Laughter,' 78.

66  Joyce, *Ulysses,* 37.

67  The relation of the self to the self's own ghost is a common Romantic trope, leading to a new sense that the self can be simultaneously multiple and whole. In his verse dialogue 'Phantom or Fact?' Coleridge writes: 'A lovely form there sate beside my bed . . . 'Twas my own spirit come from heaven.' Yet, in a striking enactment of self-alienation, his phantom shrinks back from himself with a 'disavowing look' (*The Friend,* essay 5, 10 Aug. 1809). In *The Prelude* Wordsworth's self walks with another that is both self and not-self, namely Nature. Whitman too walks with his own soul ('Oh soul, repressless, I with thee and thou with me'). And later, in conversation with Ibsen, Archer speculates that after the final curtain in *Ghosts,* if Mrs Alving 'did not "come to the rescue" it was no doubt the result of a *gengangere,* a ghost, still "walking in her"' (112). Here too the notion that one walks with a ghost implies self-alienation. See Archer, 'Ibsen as I Knew Him,' in *William Archer on Ibsen,* 112.

68  See Quigley, *The Modern Stage and Other Worlds,* 115–41.

69  Joyce, 'Epilogue to Ibsen's "Ghosts,"' in *The Critical Writings of James Joyce,* 271.

70  See 'The Decay of Lying,' 981. Max Beerbohm would later identify the opening scene of *Earnest* with that of *Hamlet,* comparing their theatrical effectiveness (in Ellmann, *Oscar Wilde,* 430n). And, like Hamlet, Jack Worthing is dressed in deep mourning.

71  Wilde, 'The Decay of Lying,' 986.

72  Wilde, 'The Critic as Artist,' 1026.

73  Wilde, *The Picture of Dorian Gray,* 21, 32, 53, 74.

74  Wilde, 'The Fisherman and His Soul,' 255.

75  Wilde, *The Picture of Dorian Gray,* 119.

76  Wilde, *Salomé,* 553.

77  Ibid., 562–3, emphasis added.
78  Scarry, *The Body in Pain*, 206.
79  Kant, *Critique of Judgment*, #16, p. 77; #2, p. 46.
80  Wilde, 'The Soul of Man under Socialism,' 1087.
81  Wilde, *Salomé*, 574. See, in *Hamlet*, Claudius: 'Give me some light' (3.2.269).
82  Riquelme, 'Shalom/Solomon/*Salomé*,' 583–4. Also for a 'feminist' reading, see Kramer, 'Cultural and Musical Hermeneutics,' 269–94. For a reading of the play as both Romantic and pictorial, see Conrad, *Romantic Opera*.
83  Bernhardt, *The Art of the Theatre*, 137.
84  Wilde, 'The Fisherman and His Soul,' 260.
85  Abrams, *The Mirror and the Lamp*, 48.
86  Wilde, 'The Critic as Artist,' 1027.
87  Hegel, *Introductory Lectures*, lecture 1: II.
88  See Ellmann, *Oscar Wilde*, 220.
89  Hegel, *Introductory Lectures*, lecture 1: II–III.
90  Joyce, *The Critical Writings*, 205. The first production of the English Players, a troupe founded by Joyce and the English actor Claud Sykes for the purpose of putting on plays in Switzerland in 1918, was *The Importance of Being Earnest*.
91  Hegel, *Introductory Lectures*, lecture 1: XIV.
92  Hegel, *Hegel's Logic*, 190.
93  Goethe, *Theory of Colour*, 57.
94  Pater, *The Renaissance*, xix.
95  Stevens, 'An Ordinary Evening in New Haven,' 331.

## Chapter 3:  Samuel Beckett's *spectres du noir*

1  Perez, *The Material Ghost*, 119–20.
2  Keaton's use of the medium may evoke what Michael Fried has called the 'facingness' of Manet's paintings, the provocative frontal gaze they direct, through a single figure, at the beholder. In the development of pictorial modernism, Fried says, Manet reconfigures the relation between painting and observer in paintings that face the beholder as never before. This acknowledgment of the beholder is the 'key to Manet's pictures' notorious "flatness."' The *tableau* is simultaneously 'antitheatrical and theatrical' (*Manet's Modernism*, 265–70).
3  Beckett, *Collected Shorter Plays*, 167.
4  Beckett, *Three Novels*, 280. All further references to *Molloy, Malone Dies,* or *The Unnamable* will be to this edition (1955) of *Three Novels*.
5  Scarry, *Dreaming by the Book*, 5, original emphasis.

6  Beckett, 'A Piece of Monologue,' in *Collected Shorter Plays*, 267.

7  Beckett, *Three Novels*, 26, 14.

8  Aristotle had instructed the poet to follow the example of good portrait painters (*Poetics*, 82), but Diderot has been the seminal thinker for modern
theories of painting and theatre, as several major studies have shown.
These include Michael Fried's *Absorption and Theatricality*, Martin Meisel's
*Realizations*, and Joseph Roach's *The Player's Passion*. Fried's influence on more
recent works in theatre studies can be seen, for instance, in W.B. Worthen,
*Modern Drama and the Rhetoric of Theater*. Worthen claims that modern dramatists' imagining the stage in pictorial terms has enabled the theatre to assume
a 'double shape' as simultaneously a 'theater of disclosure and also a theater
of concealment' (27–8). Among numerous late-nineteenth- and early-
twentieth-century instances of this pictorial dramaturgy in English, key
articulations include *The Principles of Playmaking*, in which Brander Matthews
argued that the stage had undergone a transformation in the mid-nineteenth
century so that 'the curtain rose and fell in a picture-frame. The characters
of the play were thereafter elements in a picture ... The drama immediately
became more pictorial' (236–7). And William Archer had employed a similar analogy in *Play-Making* to make an explicitly antitheatrical argument.
Thinking of the stage in 'pictorial terms,' the playwright can guard against
'theatricality' (13). 'The stage now aims at presenting a complete picture.' The
picture has depth, and characters are set 'completely in it' (64).

9  Beckett, quotation from *Unnamable* in *Three Novels*, 293; Beckett quoted in
Fletcher and Spurling, *Beckett*, 25.

10  Beckett, *First Love and Other Shorts*, 70, 71.

11  Szondi, *Theory of the Modern Drama*, 16.

12  Maeterlinck, 'Le tragique quotidien,' 187–8.

13  Hegel, *Introductory Lectures*, 1: XIV.

14  See especially M.H. Abrams's seminal studies *The Mirror and the Lamp* and
*Natural Supernaturalism*; also Jean-Marie Schaeffer's critique of that tradition in *Art of the Modern Age* and Rodolphe Gasché's *The Tain of the Mirror*.

15  Meisel, *Realizations*, 7.

16  Pirandello, *Six Characters*, 49.

17  Stanislavski, *My Life in Art*, 463; *An Actor Prepares*, 136; *Building a
Character*, 37–8.

18  Dumas, *Théâtre complet*, 208–9.

19  Michael Fried responds directly to this way of thinking in his famous
polemic 'Art and Objecthood,' when he writes of a war going on (in the
1960s) between the theatrical and the pictorial. '*The success, even survival of
the arts has come increasingly to depend on their ability to defeat theater*. This is

perhaps nowhere more evident than within theater itself, where the need
to defeat what I have been calling theater has chiefly made itself felt as the
need to establish a drastically different relation to its audience' (in *Art and
Objecthood*, 153).

20  Sarcey, *Essai d'une esthétique de théâtre*, 1: 125–7, 129.
21  Meisel, *Realizations*, 44.
22  States, *Great Reckonings*, 5–6.
23  Roach, *The Player's Passion*, 216.
24  Carlson, *The Haunted Stage*, 2, 13.
25  Schaeffer, *Art of the Modern Age*, 284.
26  Beckett, 'Three Dialogues,' in *Disjecta*, 145.
27  Beckett, *Unnamable*, 350.
28  Beckett, *Lessness*, 8.
29  Beckett, *How It Is*, 28.
30  Kenner, *Samuel Beckett*, 10.
31  *Still* is illustrated with three engravings and three preliminary studies by
Stanley William Hayter.
32  There have been important studies in which critics have argued that
Beckett achieves what Richard Begam calls 'a fully perfected act of nonrep-
resentation or antiexpression' (*Samuel Beckett and the End of Modernity*, 8).
For an excellent account of the anti-expressive aims that Beckett describes
in 'Three Dialogues,' see Daniel Albright's *Representation and Imagination*.
Yet Albright treats the 'Three Dialogues' as 'the culmination of a long tradition of denunciations of self-expression, including Matthew Arnold's
1853 preface' (160), a position that, in my view, Beckett would contest,
especially insofar as his work is seen to extend the Romantic form–content
dialectic. Moreover, Albright's argument, like some other outstanding examples of Beckett criticism, focuses principally on a problem of language
(in this case, specifically on writing) and does not adequately address the
fact that Beckett is writing about painting and that important homologies
exist between painting and theatre. Leo Bersani and Ulysse Dutoit, in their
brilliant *Arts of Impoverishment*, read Beckett in conjunction with painter
Mark Rothko and filmmaker Alain Resnais. In different forms, those three
renounce art's authority by challenging boundaries between art and the
world, between subject and object, as well as those between what Beckett
calls, in 'Three Dialogues,' 'representer and representee.' Beckett, Rothko,
and Resnais 'refuse to serve the complacency of a culture that expects art
to reinforce its moral and epistemological authority' (8). However, also
focusing on Beckett's non-theatrical prose, Bersani and Dutoit practise
a kind of speculative or Hegelian metaphysics. In *Company*, they argue,

'what cannot be thought, and what thought flees from, is the identity of consciousness with itself' (*Arts of Impoverishment*, 68). Stanley Cavell reads Beckett as a paragon of anti-theatricality, a kind of positivist who presents a literalness that subverts the tendency of his audience to read between the lines. Cavell too focuses on 'the language Beckett has discovered or invented; not now its use in dialogue, but its grammar, its particular way of making sense, especially the quality it has of what I will call *hidden literality*. The words strew obscurities across our path and seem willfully to thwart comprehension; and then time after time we discover that their meaning has been missed only because it was so utterly bare – totally, therefore unnoticeably, in view. Such a discovery has the effect of show-ing us that it is *we* who had been willfully uncomprehending, misleading ourselves in demanding further, or other, meaning where the meaning was nearest' ('End the Waiting Game,' 119–20). It must be acknowledged that Cavell proceeds, ironically perhaps, to deliver an extraordinary, mi-drashic interpretation of *Endgame*. Citing Cavell, among others, Bersani and Dutoit remark on the 'agreement among critics of quite different interests and levels of insights, of how *expressive* Beckett's work is' (*Arts of Impoverishment*, 13). The present essay is indebted to many who have come before, but especially to Bersani and Dutoit, and Cavell.

33 Beckett, *Murphy*, 248, 246. Later, Murphy's imagining of the disturbing non-flatness of Endon's eyeballs explicitly evokes Buñuel slitting the eyeball of a young woman with a razor blade in his film *Un chien andalou* (1928). Just before his death, Murphy 'lay down in a tuft of soaking tuf-fets ... He saw eyeballs being scraped, first any eyeballs, then Mr Endon's' (251). The reader may recognize the allusion, but, for Murphy himself, it is only one of many fragmented images, 'evoking nothing.'

34 White, *Figural Realism*, 66, 70.

35 Quoted in Rosenberg and Myers, *Echoes from the Holocaust*, 41. Also recall George Steiner's famous remark: 'The world of Auschwitz lies outside speech as it lies outside reason' (quoted in Lang, *Act and Idea in the Nazi Genocide*, 151). In 'Kulturkritik und Gesellschaft' (1949, pub. 1951), Adorno famously commented: 'After Auschwitz, to write a poem is barbaric.' (Nach Auschwitz ein Gedicht zu schreiben ist barbarisch.) John Felstiner provides a detailed history of this statement in 'Translating Paul Celan's "Todesfuge,"' in *Probing the Limits of Representation*, 242.

36 Beckett, 'Three Dialogues,' in *Disjecta*, 139.

37 White, *Figural Representation*, 79.

38 In *L'imaginaire* Sartre distinguishes between perception and imagining or imaging consciousness: 'The image is an act that aims at an absent or

nonexistent object in its corporeality by means of a physical or psychical content that is given not for its own sake but only as an "analogical representative" of the intended object' (45). The imaging consciousness has an important moral and historical dimension in Sartre. (Cf. Flynn, 'Sartre and the Poetics of History,' 213–60.) For the discussion of *l'en soi,* see Sartre's *Being and Nothingness.* In aiming to put 'essences back into existence,' Maurice Merleau-Ponty writes, 'Truth does not inhabit only the "inner man," or more accurately, there is no inner man, man is in the world, and only in the world does he know himself' (*Phenomenology of Perception,* xi). Sartre and Merleau-Ponty were editors of *Les Temps Modernes* (in which the article by Levinas, discussed below, was published) in the years following the war.

39  For Heidegger's influence on Merleau-Ponty and Sartre, see Moran, *Introduction to Phenomenology,* 412.

40  Beckett, 'La peinture des van Velde,' in *Disjecta,* 118.

41  Heidegger, 'The Origin of the Work of Art,' 161.

42  Levinas, 'Réalité et son ombre,' 771, 773.

43  Heidegger, 'The Origin of the Work of Art,' 197.

44  Levinas, 'Réalité et son ombre,' 775.

45  Derrida, *The Truth in Painting,* 258.

46  Ibid., 329–31.

47  It is difficult to pinpoint exactly when piles of shoes became an iconic image of the Holocaust. Photographs of piles of shoes among other remains were taken upon liberation of the camps by different Allied forces. These liberation photographs were shown at the Nuremberg trials, as well as appearing in newsreel footage shown in Europe and the United States. Also, at the war's end, makeshift memorials were set up at camps in Poland (for instance, at Majdanek and Auschwitz); shoes and other material objects (prison uniforms, luggage, eyeglasses, etc.) were left in place to serve as the first memorials to those who perished. See Young, *The Texture of Memory,* 124, 132. Shoes were also a popular symbol among Jewish writers during the war. Abraham Sutzkever, the great Yiddish poet, wrote a poem entitled 'A Wagon of Shoes' in the Vilna ghetto in 1943: 'I must not ask you *whose,* / My heart, it skips a beat: / Tell me the truth, oh, shoes, / Where disappeared the feet?' Also see Ellen Carol Jones's essay 'Empty Shoes,' which chronicles the image of the 'empty' shoes of Holocaust victims as presented in post-Holocaust art, literature, and memorials. And see Amishai-Maisels, *Depiction and Interpretation,* 148–51, for a discussion of the use of 'relics' such as shoes in Holocaust-related art. The author cites particularly a 1962 painting by Marc Klionsky entitled 'Pile of Shoes.' I am

indebted to Rona Sheramy for sharing her wide-ranging knowledge of Holocaust history.

48 Beckett, *Waiting for Godot*, 37. Responding to what he calls the 'duel' between Meyer Schapiro and Heidegger, Derrida notes: 'All of you seem too sure of what you call internal description. And the external never remains outside. What's at stake here is a decision about the frame, about what separates the internal from the external, with a border which is itself double in its trait, and joins what it splits' (*The Truth in Painting*, 331).

49 Beckett, *Endgame*, 33.

50 Kristeva, 'Modern Theater Does Not Take (A) Place,' 131.

51 Beckett, 'Three Dialogues,' in *Disjecta*, 145.

52 Greenberg, 'Modernist Painting,' 87.

53 Ibid., 90.

54 Valency, *The End of the World*, 389. Daniel Albright also links Beckett to nineteenth-century symbolism, invoking Beckett's own essay on Proust in which Beckett uses the term 'autosymbolism' (*Representation and Imagination*, 169). It is problematic, however, to use Beckett's early essay on another writer to define the aims of his own, mature work, unless one were to say, following Harold Bloom, that Beckett misreads Proust 'so as to clear imaginative space for [himself]' (*Anxiety of Influence*, 5). Beckett had written: 'For Proust the object may be a living symbol, but a symbol of itself. The symbolism of Baudelaire has become *autosymbolism* in Proust' (*Proust*, 60).

55 Fried, 'Shape as Form,' in *Art and Objecthood*, 78.

56 Beckett, *Unnamable*, 340.

57 Beckett, 'Peintres de l'empêchement,' in *Disjecta*, 136.

58 Begam, *Samuel Beckett and the End of Modernity*, 110.

59 Beckett, 'Peintres de l'empêchement,' in *Disjecta*, 136.

60 I thank Jonathan Warren for helping me to translate and to understand Beckett's essay.

61 Beckett, *Molloy*, 10.

62 Beckett, *Endgame*, 44, 81.

63 Beckett, *Molloy*, 113.

64 'La peinture des van Velde ou le monde et le pantalon,' also 1948, is a more developed version of 'Peintres de l'empêchement'; both reject conventional understandings of subject–object relations. The former also supplies a crucial anecdote on the theme of artistic making to *Endgame*. As for the rejection of philosophical reflection, Derrida is careful to explain that dissemination is written on the back of the mirror. 'Not on its inverted specter.' I do not want simply to conflate Beckett's and Derrida's images, yet it must

be stressed that Beckett's *spectre* is also importantly *not* a spectre in any spiritual or reflective sense. Again my aim is, at least in part, to historicize the trope of ghosts that haunts the oeuvres of both Beckett and Derrida. See Derrida, *Dissemination*, 33.

65  Garner, 'Visual Field in Beckett's Late Plays,' 350–1. Garner does effectively call attention to 'the aesthetic surface of visual abstraction' in Beckett and the way Beckett 'undermines the effect of depth, rendering the third dimension of his performance images unstable' (*Bodied Spaces*, 63, 74). However, Garner is not primarily interested in the fact of flatness or in flatness as a motif but, following Merleau-Ponty and art historians such as Rudolf Arnheim, in the interaction of the image and the intelligent eye. To my mind, the project of reading Beckett through the lens of individual philosophers is always in danger of oversimplifying. And, though both Garner and, more recently, Lois Oppenheim note striking parallels in the works of Beckett and Merleau-Ponty, Beckett's complexity as an artist seems reduced in the process.

66  Beckett is responding here to an old theoretical debate about the temporality of 'non-kinetic' arts. Like Joyce in both Stephen's aesthetic theory in *A Portrait* and the 'Proteus' chapter of *Ulysses*, Beckett can be read against Lessing, especially *Laocoön: An Essay on the Limits of Painting and Poetry*. For Beckett's contemporaries, on temporality and painting, see Souriau, 'Time in the Plastic Arts,' and Arnheim, 'Space as an Image of Time.' For my own understanding of the topic, I am also indebted to Meisel, 'The Moment's Story: Painting,' in *Realizations*, 17–28.

67  Beckett, *Proust*, 55–6, 19, 46–7.

68  Beckett, *Murphy*, 107, 4, emphasis added.

69  Stanley Cavell writes: 'It is the nature of hearing that what is heard comes from someplace, whereas what you can see you can look at. It is why sounds are warnings, or calls; it is why our access to another world is normally through voices from it; and why a man can be spoken to by God and survive, but not if he sees God, in which case he is no longer in this world. Whereas we are not accustomed to seeing things that are invisible, or not present to us, not present with us; or we are not accustomed to acknowledging that we do (except for dreams). Yet this seems, ontologically, to be what is happening when we look at a photograph: we see things that are not present' (*The World Viewed*, 18). Beckett's *Film*, of course, is silent, and he seems to have realized precisely the point that Cavell is making and to be responding to it.

70  Cavell, *The World Viewed*, 24.

71  Chaplin quoted in Robinson, *Chaplin*, 459.

72  Beckett, *Film,* in *Collected Shorter Plays,* 163.

73  Beckett, *Molloy,* 108.

74  Kermode, *Romantic Image,* 47.

75  Kandinsky, *Concerning the Spiritual in Art,* 75.

76  Beckett, 'Three Dialogues,' in *Disjecta,* 144. I take the modifier 'every man his own wife' to signify the old notion that 'beauty is in the eye of the beholder' or the failed aim of the painter to be true to his own supposed vision.

77  Ibid., 145.

78  Ibid.; Beckett, *Endgame,* 70.

79  Beckett, 'Imagination Dead Imagine,' in *First Love and Other Shorts,* 63, 66.

80  Illig, 'Acting Beckett's Women,' 26.

81  Beckett, *Eh Joe,* in *Collected Shorter Plays,* 202, 203.

82  The television is conventionally figured as a box in which viewers are 'absorbed.' A popular fantasy is that scenario in which ghosts in the machine draw the viewer into the television itself, as in Stephen Spielberg's *Poltergeist* (1982).

83  Knowlson, *Damned to Fame,* 476.

84  Beckett, *The Lost Ones,* 7, emphasis added.

85  Ibid., 30–3.

86  Beckett, notebook 5, 14 February 1937; quoted in Knowlson, *Damned to Fame,* 238.

87  Quoted in Harvey, *Samuel Beckett,* 433–4.

88  Quoted in Knowlson, *Damned to Fame,* 548.

89  Beckett, *Collected Shorter Prose,* 253–4.

90  Brater, *Beyond Minimalism,* 87.

91  Turits, 'Moment of Impact,' 34.

92  Beckett, *Murphy,* 4.

93  Beckett, 'Peintres de l'empêchement,' in *Disjecta,* 136.

94  Beckett, *Ghost Trio,* in *Collected Shorter Plays,* 248.

95  Beckett, *Molloy,* 88.

96  Begam, *Samuel Beckett and the End of Modernity,* 103, 83.

97  Beckett, *Molloy,* 145.

98  Beckett, *Ghost Trio,* 250.

99  Ibid., 253.

100  Ibid., 252.

101  Beckett, *Disjecta,* 22.

102  Beckett, *The Lost Ones,* 55.

103  Beckett, *Malone Dies,* 282.

104  Beckett, *The Lost Ones,* 28.

105 Identifying ghosts as a key motif in modern literature, Jean-Michel Rabaté
    seeks to extend Harold Bloom's famous model, in Beckett's case, with a
    Freudian analysis of the 'positivity of "nothing."' Yet in claiming that
    'Beckett staunchly identifies art with truth' and that in Beckett (the author
    and the works), the heart 'represents the point of connection between
    the body and soul,' Rabaté betrays a Hegelian optimism that so much of
    Beckett's work appears to reject. See Rabaté, *The Ghosts of Modernity*, 154–5.
106 Beckett, *Endgame*, 55.
107 Deane, *Strange Country*, 95.
108 Joyce, *Ulysses*, 91.
109 Beckett, 'Dante . . . Bruno . . Vico . Joyce,' in *Disjecta*, 23–4, 27, 33.
110 Greenblatt, *Hamlet in Purgatory*, 61.
111 Beckett, 'Assumption,' in *Complete Short Prose*, 6.
112 Beckett, 'A Piece of Monologue,' in *Collected Shorter Plays*, 266, 269.
113 Joyce, *Ulysses*, 498.
114 Beckett, *Malone Dies*, 210.
115 Beckett, *En attendant Godot*, 16.
116 Barthes, *On Racine*, viii, original emphasis.
117 Racine, *Athalie*, 60.
118 Beckett, *Endgame*, 34.

## Chapter 4: The Spirit of Toys

  1 See Roland Barthes on French toys imitating Nature: 'There exist, for
    instance, dolls that urinate; they have an oesophagus, one gives them
    a bottle, they wet their nappies; soon, no doubt, milk will turn to water
    in their stomachs' (*Mythologies*, 53). And puppets have eaten, had sex,
    and died in puppet shows at least from the Grand-Guignol to Federico
    Garcia Lorca's *La tragicomedia de don Cristóbal* (1931) to Ronnie Burkett's
    *Happy* (2000). Lois Rostow Kuznet has written broadly on animated toys
    in literature which, unlike 'real-world' toys, represent 'not only human
    hopes, needs, and desires, but human anxieties and terrors as well' (*When
    Toys Come Alive*, 1). Toys have had a historical relationship, though a
    complicated one, to objects of religious ritual (such as the crèches of nativ-
    ity scenes); largely such objects were forbidden children. For a historical
    survey of toys in Western culture, see Fraser, *A History of Toys*. Largely,
    writing on toys and children's literature (see, e.g., Lurie, *The Subversive
    Power of Children's Literature*, and Fox, *The Doll*) assumes a romantic qual-
    ity, whereby children are regarded as little noble savages living a kind of
    pastoral innocence opposed to the sexually, economically, politically driven
    world of grown-ups. This last view is one that I especially want to contest.

2 http://disney.go.com/disneyvideos/animatedfilms/toystory/characters/
mutant.htm.

3 Turner, *Drama, Fields, and Metaphors*, 273.

4 For a detailed account of the Pixar–Disney relationship, see Price, *The Pixar
Touch*, 117–24. In Paik and Iwerks, *To Infinity and Beyond!* the studio hon-
ours its own history, with forewords by the key players, such as Lasseter
and Jobs, and a broad survey of Pixar's 'triumphs.' Also see http://www.
pixar.com/companyinfo/history/1984.html.

5 Baudelaire, 'A Philosophy of Toys,' 203; 'Morale du joujou,' 207.

6 See Comay, 'Materialist Mutations of the Bilderverbot,' 353–5.

7 Marx, *Capital*, 1: 163–5.

8 Benjamin, 'On Some Motifs,' 188; 'The Work of Art,' 220–2.

9 I refer to 'chapters' as labelled on the DVDs.

10 For another explicit instance, see the toys' arrival at the door of Al's Toy
Barn, where they see the sign 'Closed,' which one character reads aloud
only to be reprimanded that the other toys aren't 'preschoolers' and that
they 'can read.' They enter in any case.

11 This particular encrypting has anticipated one of the most important recent
technical developments in film. In *Final Fantasy: The Spirits Within*, characters
from a video game have been transferred into the medium of film through
digital computerization. Rick Lyman reports that 'film-makers are beginning to create photo-realistic computer characters that, at least in fleeting
moments, will try to persuade the audience that actual humans are on the
screen. It is called photo-realistic animation.' See Lyman, 'Movie Stars,' 1, 16.

12 Price, *The Pixar Touch*, 134.

13 Comay, 'Krapp and Other Matters,' n.p.

14 Koppman note in Katschke, *Toy Story 2*, n.p.

15 Comay, 'Krapp and Other Matters,' n.p.

16 Joyce, *Ulysses*, 45.

17 http:// disney.go.com/disneyvideos/animatedfilms/toystory/about/abfilm
.htm.

18 Kanfer, *Serious Business*, 229.

19 Price, *The Pixar Touch*, 151.

20 John Donne writes in the second of his holy sonnets:

> . . . O God, first was I made
> By thee, and for thee, and when I was decay'd
> Thy blood bought that, the which before was thine.

21 This limited point-of-view shot, a doubled seeing shared by character and
audience, was pioneered by Jean Renoir in *Boudu Saved from Drowning*
(1932), in which a Paris bookseller, looking from his window through a

telescope thinks he sees the title character attempting suicide by jumping into the Seine.

22  See, specifically, Hieronymous Bosch's 'Vision of the Otherworld,' a late-fifteenth-century panel that depicts cleansed souls lifted by angels towards what Stephen Greenblatt has described as 'a long funnel, a kind of birth canal, at whose end figures are emerging into a blinding light' (*Hamlet in Purgatory*, 59). I also draw on Greenblatt's brilliant treatment of purgatory as a 'poet's fable' and his discussion of relations between purgatory, resurrection, ghosts, dreams, and theatre.

23  http://disney.go.com/vault/archives/characters/woody/woody.html.

24  Perez, *The Material Ghost*, 34.

25  Bercovitch, *Puritan Origins*, 87.

26  Lukács, *History and Class Consciousness*, 84.

27  Beckett, *Proust*, 20.

28  Smith, *The Total Work of Art*, 169.

# Works Cited

Abrams, M.H. *The Mirror and the Lamp: Romantic Theory and the Critical Tradition.* London: Oxford University Press, 1953.
– *Natural Supernaturalism: Tradition and Revolution in Romantic Literature.* New York: W.W. Norton & Co., 1971.
Ackerman, Alan. 'The Prompter's Box: Back to the Future: One Hundred Years after Ibsen.' *Modern Drama* 49, no. 3 (2006): 225–34.
– 'Visualizing Hamlet's Ghost: The Rise of Modern Subjectivity.' *Theatre Journal* 53 (2001): 119–44.
Albright, Daniel. *Representation and Imagination: Beckett, Kafka, Nabokov, and Schoenberg.* Chicago: University of Chicago Press, 1981.
Amishai-Maisels, Ziva. *Depiction and Interpretation: The Influence of the Holocaust on the Visual Arts.* New York: Pergamon Press, 1993.
Archer, William. *Play-Making.* New York: Dodd, Mead, 1912.
– *Play-Making: A Manual of Craftsmanship.* London: Chapman & Hall, 1913.
– Preface. *Ibsen's Prose Dramas.* New York: Charles Scribner's Sons, 1980.
– *William Archer on Ibsen: The Major Essays, 1889–1919.* Edited by Thomas Postlewait. London: Greenwood Press, 1984.
Arnheim, Rudolf. 'Space as an Image of Time.' In *Images of Romanticism: Verbal and Visual Affinities,* edited by Karl Kroeber and William Walling, 1–12. New Haven: Yale University Press, 1978.
– *Visual Thinking.* Berkeley: University of California Press, 1969.
Aristotle. *Poetics.* Translated by S.H. Butcher. New York: Hill & Wang, 1961.
Auerbach, Erich. *Mimesis: The Representation of Reality in Western Literature.* Translated by Willard R. Trask. Princeton: Princeton University Press, 1953.
Baird, Daniel. 'Screen Savers.' *Globe and Mail,* 12 December 2009, M3.
Barthes, Roland. *Mythologies.* 1957. Translated by Annette Lavers. New York: Farrar, Straus & Giroux, 1972.

– *On Racine* (1960). Translated by Richard Howard. New York: Performing Arts Journal Publications, 1983.

Baudelaire, Charles. 'Morale du joujou.' In *Oeuvres complètes*, 201–7. Paris: Librairie Gallimard, 1951.

– 'A Philosophy of Toys.' In *The Painter of Modern Life and Other Essays*, translated and edited by Jonathan Mayne, 197–203. London: Phaidon Press, 1964.

Beckett, Samuel. 'Assumption.' In *The Complete Short Prose*, edited by S.E. Gontarski, 3–7. New York: Grove Press, 1995.

– *Collected Shorter Plays*. London: Faber & Faber, 1984.

– *Disjecta: Miscellaneous Writings and a Dramatic Fragment*. Edited by Ruby Cohn. New York: Grove Press, 1984.

– *En attendant Godot*. Paris: Les Éditions de minuit, 1952.

– *Endgame*. New York: Grove Press, 1958.

– *Fin de partie*. Paris: Les Éditions de minuit, 1957.

– *First Love and Other Shorts*. New York: Grove Press, 1974.

– *How It Is*. New York: Grove Press, 1964.

– *Lessness*. London: Calder & Boyars, 1970.

– *The Lost Ones*. New York: Grove Press, 1972.

– *Murphy*. New York: Grove Press, 1957.

– *Proust*. New York: Grove Press, 1957.

– *Three Novels*. New York: Grove Press, 1955.

– *Waiting for Godot*. New York: Grove Press, 1954.

Begam, Richard. *Samuel Beckett and the End of Modernity*. Stanford: Stanford University Press, 1996.

'Behind the Scenes.' http://disney.go.com/disneypictures/achristmascarol/#/christmas_present/ (accessed 15 January 2010).

Benjamin, Walter. 'On Some Motifs in Baudelaire.' In *Illuminations*, translated by Harry Zohn, 155–94. New York: Schocken Books, 1968.

– 'The Work of Art in the Age of Mechanical Reproduction.' In *Illuminations*, 217–51.

Bennett, Benjamin. *Modern Drama and German Classicism: Renaissance from Lessing to Brecht*. Ithaca: Cornell University Press, 1979.

Bercovitch, Sacvan. *The Puritan Origins of the American Self*. New Haven: Yale University Press, 1975.

Bergson, Henri. 'Laughter.' In *Comedy*, edited by Wylie Sypher, 61–190. Baltimore: Johns Hopkins University Press, 1956.

Berkeley, George. *A New Theory of Vision and Other Select Philosophical Writings*. London: J.M. Dent & Sons, 1910.

Bernhardt, Sarah. *The Art of the Theatre*. London: Dial Press, 1925.

Bersani, Leo, and Ulysse Dutoit. *Arts of Impoverishment: Beckett, Rothko, Resnais.* Cambridge, MA: Harvard University Press, 1993.

Bloom, Harold. *Anxiety of Influence.* London: Oxford University Press, 1973.

Bradley, A.C. *Shakespearean Tragedy.* London, 1904. Project Gutenberg, http://www.gutenberg.org/files/16966/16966-h/16966-h.htm.

Brater, Enoch. *Beyond Minimalism: Beckett's Late Style in the Theater.* New York: Oxford University Press, 1987.

Brooks, Peter. *The Melodramatic Imagination: Balzac, Henry James, Melodrama, and the Mode of Excess.* New Haven: Yale University Press, 1976.

– *Realist Vision.* New Haven: Yale University Press, 2005.

Brown, Bill. 'How to Do Things with Things (A Toy Story).' *Critical Inquiry* 24, no. 4 (Summer 1998): 935–64. http://www.jstor.org/stable/1344113.

– *A Sense of Things: The Object Matter of American Literature.* Chicago: University of Chicago Press, 2003.

– 'Thing Theory.' *Critical Inquiry* 28 (2001): 1–22.

Brustein, Robert. *Theatre of Revolt.* Chicago: Elephant Paperbacks, 1962.

Carlson, Marvin. *The Haunted Stage: The Theatre as Memory Machine.* Ann Arbor: University of Michigan Press, 2001.

Carlyle, Thomas. *Sartor Resartus.* In *Carlyle's Complete Works.* 1831. Reprinted, Boston: Estes & Lauriat, 1885.

Castle, Terry. 'Phantasmagoria: Spectral Technology and the Metaphysics of Modern Reverie.' *Critical Inquiry* 15 (1988): 26–61.

Cavell, Stanley. 'Ending the Waiting Game: A Reading of Beckett's *Endgame.*' In *Must We Mean What We Say?* 115–62. Cambridge: Cambridge University Press, 1969.

– 'Hamlet's Burden of Proof.' In *Disowning Knowledge in Six Plays of Shakespeare,* 179–92. Cambridge: Cambridge University Press, 1987.

– *The World Viewed: Reflections of the Ontology of Film.* Cambridge, MA: Harvard University Press, 1971.

Chantraine, P. *Dictionnaire étymologique de la langue grecque.* Paris: Klincksieck, 1968.

Chaudhuri, Una. *Staging Place: The Geography of Modern Drama.* Ann Arbor: University of Michigan Press, 1997.

Clay, Carolyn. Review of *Ghosts. Boston Phoenix,* 1 June 1982, n.p.

Coleridge, Samuel Taylor. *Lectures 1808–1819 on Literature.* Volume 5 [2-volume set]. *Collected Works,* edited by Reginald A. Foakes. Princeton: Princeton University Press, 1987.

– *Lectures upon Shakespeare and Other Dramatists. The Complete Works of Samuel Taylor Coleridge,* edited by W.G.T. Shedd. New York: Harper & Brothers, 1884.

Comay, Rebecca. 'Krapp and Other Matters.' Unpublished interview with
   Atom Egoyan, March 2001.
– 'Materialist Mutations of the Bilderverbot.' In *Sites of Vision: The Discursive
   Construction of Sight in the History of Philosophy*, edited by David Michael
   Levin, 337–78. Cambridge, MA: MIT Press, 1997.
Conrad, Peter. *Romantic Opera and Literary Form*. Berkeley: University of
   California Press, 1977.
Crary, Jonathan. *Techniques of the Observer: On Vision and Modernity in the
   Nineteenth Century*. Cambridge, MA: MIT Press, 1990.
Deane, Seamus. *Strange Country: Modernity and Nationhood in Irish Writing
   since 1790*. Oxford: Clarendon Press, 1997.
de Bolla, Peter. 'The Visibility of Visuality.' In *Vision in Context: Historical and
   Contemporary Perspectives on Sight*, edited by Teresa Brennan and Martin
   Jay, 63–82. New York: Routledge, 1996.
Debord, Guy Ernest. *La société du spectacle*. Paris: Éditions Champ Libre,
   1971.
Derrida, Jacques. *Dissemination*. Translated by Barbara Johnson. Chicago:
   University of Chicago Press, 1981.
– *Specters of Marx: The State of the Debt, the Work of Mourning, & the New
   International*. Translated by Peggy Kamuf. New York: Routledge, 1994.
– *The Truth in Painting*. Translated by Geoff Bennington and Ian McLeod.
   Chicago: University of Chicago Press, 1987.
Descartes, René. *Meditations*. In *The Philosophical Works of Descartes*, volume 1
   [2-volume set], translated by E.S. Haldane and G.R.T. Ross. Cambridge,
   MA: Dover, 1955.
Dickens, Charles. *A Christmas Carol*. New York: Penguin Books, 1984.
– *Great Expectations*. London: Penguin Books, 1965.
Disney. Disney Archives. 'Woody.' http://disney.go.com/vault/archives/
   characters/woody/woody.html (accessed 15 June 2005).
– *Toy Story*. 'About the Video.' http://disney.go.com/disneyvideos/
   animatedfilms/toystory/about/abfilm.htm (accessed 15 June 2005).
– *Toy Story*. 'Mutant Toys.' http://disney.go.com/disneyvideos/animatedfilms/
   toystory/characters/mutant.htm (accessed 15 June 2005).
Dolan, Jill. *Utopia in Performance: Finding Hope at the Theater*. Ann Arbor:
   University of Michigan Press, 2005.
Donne, John. *Poetical Works*. Edited by Herbert J.C. Grierson. Oxford: Oxford
   University Press, 1971.
Dowden, Edward. *Shakespeare: A Critical Study of His Mind and Art*. London:
   Routledge, 1875.

Dumas, Alexandre. *Théatre complet de Al. Dumas Fils.* 3rd series. Paris: Michel Lévy Frères, 1868.

Durbach, Errol. *Ibsen the Romantic: Analogues of Paradise in the Later Plays.* Athens: University of Georgia Press, 1982.

Eliot, T.S. 'Hamlet.' In *Selected Prose of T.S. Eliot,* edited by Frank Kermode, 45–9. New York: Farrar, Straus & Giroux, 1975.

Ellmann, Richard. *Oscar Wilde.* New York: Vintage Books, 1987.

Felstiner, John. 'Translating Paul Celan's "Todesfuge."' In *Probing the Limits of Representation: Nazism and the Final Solution,* edited by Saul Friedlander, 240–58. Cambridge, MA: Harvard University Press, 1992.

Fergusson, Francis. *The Idea of a Theater: A Study of Ten Plays, The Art of Drama in Changing Perspective.* Princeton: Princeton University Press, 1949.

Ficino, Marsilio. *Commentary on Plato's* Symposium *on Love.* Translated by Sears Jayne. Dallas: Spring Publications, 1985.

– *Theologica Platonica: De immortalitate animorum.* Hildesheim: Georg Olms Verlag, 1975.

Fletcher, John, and John Spurling. *Beckett: The Playwright.* New York: Hill & Wang, 1972.

Flynn, Thomas F. 'Sartre and the Poetics of History.' In *The Cambridge Companion to Sartre,* edited by Christina Howells, 213–60. New York: Cambridge University Press, 1992.

Foucault, Michel. *The Order of Things: An Archaeology of the Human Sciences.* New York: Vintage Books, 1973.

Fox, Carl. *The Doll.* New York: Abrams, 1972.

Frank, Joseph. *The Widening Gyre: Crisis and Mastery in Modern Literature.* New Brunswick, NJ: Rutgers University Press, 1963.

Fraser, Antonia. *A History of Toys.* Frankfurt am Main: Delacorte, 1966.

Freud, Sigmund. *The Interpretation of Dreams.* Edited and translated by James Strachey. London: Penguin Books, 1991.

– 'The Uncanny.' http://www-rohan.sdsu.edu/~amtower/uncanny.html.

Fried, Michael. *Absorption and Theatricality: Painting and Beholder in the Age of Diderot.* Chicago: University of Chicago Press, 1980.

– *Art and Objecthood: Essays and Reviews.* Chicago: University of Chicago Press, 1998.

– *Manet's Modernism.* Chicago: University of Chicago Press, 1996.

Frye, Northrop. *Northrop Frye on Shakespeare.* Edited by Robert Sandler. New Haven: Yale University Press, 1986.

Gadamer, Hans-Georg. *Truth and Method.* Translated by Joel Weinsheimer and Donald G. Marshall. New York: Continuum, 1995.

Ganz, Arthur. *Realms of the Self: Variations on a Theme in Modern Drama*. New York: New York University Press, 1980.

Garber, Marjorie. *Shakespeare's Ghost Writers: Literature as Uncanny Causality*. London: Methuen, 1988.

Garner, Stanton B., Jr. *Bodied Spaces: Phenomenology and Performance in Contemporary Drama*. Ithaca: Cornell University Press, 1994.

– 'Visual Field in Beckett's Late Plays.' *Comparative Drama* 21 (Winter 1987–8): 349–73.

Gasché, Rodolphe. *The Tain of the Mirror: Derrida and the Philosophy of Reflection*. Cambridge, MA: Harvard University Press, 1986.

Goethe, Johann Wolfgang von. *The Sorrows of Young Werther*. Translated by Elizabeth Mayer and Louise Bogan. New York: Vintage Books, 1990.

– *Theory of Colours*. 1810. Translated by Charles Lock Eastlake, 1840. Reprinted, London: Frank Cass, 1967.

– *Wilhelm Meister's Apprenticeship*. Translated by Eric A. Blackall. In *Goethe's Collected Works*, volume 9. Princeton: Princeton University Press, 1989.

Granville-Barker, Harley. *Prefaces to Shakespeare*. London: Sidgwick & Jackson, 1937.

Graziosi, Barbara. *Inventing Homer: The Early Reception of Epic*. New York: Cambridge University Press, 2002.

Greenberg, Clement. 'Modernist Painting.' In *The Collected Essays and Criticism*, volume 4, *Modernism with a Vengeance: 1957–1969*, edited by John O'Brien, 85–93. Chicago: University of Chicago Press, 1993.

Greenblatt, Stephen. *Hamlet in Purgatory*. Princeton: Princeton University Press, 2001.

– *Marvelous Possessions: The Wonder of the New World*. Chicago: University of Chicago Press, 1991.

– *Renaissance Self-Fashioning: From More to Shakespeare*. Chicago: University of Chicago Press, 1980.

Harvey, Lawrence E. *Samuel Beckett: Poet and Critic*. Princeton: Princeton University Press, 1970.

Hayman, Ronald. *Brecht: A Biography*. New York: Oxford University Press, 1983.

Heaney, Seamus. 'Station Island.' In *Station Island*, 61–94. New York: Farrar, Straus & Giroux, 1985.

Hegel, G.W.F. *Hegel's Logic*. Translated by William Wallace. Oxford: Oxford University Press, 1975.

– *Introductory Lectures on Aesthetics*. Translated by Bernard Bosanquet, 1886. Reprinted, London: Penguin Books, 1993.

– *The Phenomenology of Mind*. Translated by J.B. Baillie. New York: Harper & Row, 1967.

Heidegger, Martin. 'The Origin of the Work of Art.' In *Basic Writings*, edited and translated by David Farrell Krell. New York: HarperCollins, 1977.

Heller, Erich. *The Artist's Journey into the Interior and Other Essays*. New York: Random House, 1965.

Hillman, David. 'Visceral Knowledge: Shakespeare, Skepticism, and the Interior of the Early Modern Body.' In *The Body in Parts: Fantasies of Corporeality in Early Modern Europe*, edited by David Hillman and Carla Mazzio, 81–106. New York: Routledge, 1997.

Homer. *The Odyssey*. Edited by Bernard Knox. Translated by Robert Fagles. New York: Penguin, 2006.

Husserl, Edmund. *Grundprobleme der Phänomenologie*. 1910/11. Dordrecht, the Netherlands: Martinus Nijhoff, 1977.

Ibsen, Henrik. *The Complete Major Prose Plays*. Translated by Rolf Fjelde. New York: Farrar, Straus & Giroux, 1965.

– *Et Dukkehjem*. Copenhagen: Gyldendalske Boghandels Forlag, F. Hegel & Son, 1880.

Illig, Nancy. 'Acting Beckett's Women.' In *Women in Beckett: Performance and Critical Perspectives*, edited by Linda Ben-Zvi, 24–6. Urbana: University of Illinois Press, 1990.

Iser, Wolfgang. *The Fictive and the Imaginary: Charting Literary Anthropology*. Baltimore: Johns Hopkins University Press, 1993.

Jackson, Shannon. *Professing Performance: Theatre in the Academy from Philology to Performativity*. New York: Cambridge University Press, 2004.

Johnson, Barbara. *Persons and Things*. Cambridge, MA: Harvard University Press, 2008.

Johnston, Brian. *The Ibsen Cycle: The Design of the Plays from* Pillars of Society *to* When We Dead Awaken. Boston: Twayne, 1974.

Jones, Ann Rosalind, and Peter Stallybrass. *Renaissance Clothing and the Materials of Memory*. Cambridge: Cambridge University Press, 2000.

Jones, Ellen Carol. 'Empty Shoes.' In *Footnotes: On Shoes*, edited by Shari Benstock and Suzanne Ferriss, 197–232. New Brunswick, NJ: Rutgers University Press, 2001.

Jowett, B. 'Introduction.' In *The Symposium of Plato*, 5–23. Boston: Branden, 1983.

Joyce, James. *The Critical Writings of James Joyce*. Edited by Ellsworth Mason and Richard Ellmann. Ithaca: Cornell University Press, 1959.

– *Ulysses*. 1922. Reprinted, London: Penguin, 1992.

Judovitz, Dalia. 'Vision, Representation, and Technology in Descartes.' In *Modernity and the Hegemony of Vision*, edited by David Michael Levin, 63–86. Berkeley: University of California Press, 1993.

Kandinsky, Wassily. *Concerning the Spiritual in Art, and Painting in Particular.* Translated by M.T.H. Sadler. Revised by F. Golffing, M. Harrison, and F. Ostertag. New York: Wittenborn, 1970.

Kanfer, Stefan. *Serious Business: The Art and Commerce of Animation in America from Betty Boop to Toy Story.* New York: Scribner, 1997.

Kant, Immanuel. *Critique of Judgment.* Translated by Werner S. Pluhar. Indianapolis: Hackett, 1987.

– *Critique of Pure Reason.* Translated by Werner S. Pluhar. Indianapolis: Hackett, 1996.

Kaplan, Louis. *The Strange Case of William Mumler, Spirit Photographer.* Minneapolis: University of Minnesota Press, 2008.

Katschke, Judy. *Toy Story 2: Howdy, Sheriff Woody!* New York: Disney Press, 1999.

Kenner, Hugh. *Samuel Beckett: A Critical Study.* New York: Grove Press, 1961.

Kermode, Frank. *Romantic Image.* London: Routledge & Kegan Paul, 1957.

Kern, Stephen. *The Culture of Time and Space, 1880–1918.* Cambridge, MA: Harvard University Press, 1983.

Knowlson, James. *Damned to Fame: The Life of Samuel Beckett.* New York: Simon & Schuster, 1996.

Kramer, Larry. 'Cultural and Musical Hermeneutics: The Salome Complex.' *Cambridge Opera Journal* 2 (1990): 269–94.

Kristeva, Julia. 'Modern Theater Does Not Take (A) Place.' *Sub-Stance* 18/19 (1977): 131–4.

Kuznet, Lois Rostow. *When Toys Come Alive: Narratives of Animation, Metamorphosis, and Development.* New Haven: Yale University Press, 1994.

Lacan, Jacques. *The Four Fundamental Concepts of Psycho-Analysis.* Translated by Alan Sheridan, 1973. Reprinted, New York: W.W. Norton & Co., 1981.

Lamb, Charles. *Charles Lamb on Shakespeare.* Edited by Joan Coldwell. Buckinghamshire: Colin Smythe, 1978.

Lang, Berel. *Act and Idea in the Nazi Genocide.* Chicago: University of Chicago Press, 1990.

Leggatt, Alexander. *Shakespeare's Comedy of Love.* London: Methuen, 1974.

Lessing, Gotthold Ephraim. *Laocoön: An Essay on the Limits of Painting and Poetry.* Translated by Edward Allen McCormick. Baltimore: Johns Hopkins University Press, 1984.

Levin, David Michael. 'Introduction.' In *Modernity and the Hegemony of Vision,* 1–29. Berkeley: University of California Press, 1993.

Levinas, Emanuel. 'Réalité et son ombre.' *Les Temps Modernes* 38 (1948): 771–89.

Liddell, H.G., and R. Scott. *A Greek-English Lexicon.* Revised edition, edited by Sir Henry Stuart-Jones. Oxford: Clarendon Press, 1968.

Locke, John. *An Essay Concerning Human Understanding*. London: S. Birt,
S. Browne, et al., 1753.

Löwith, Karl. *From Hegel to Nietzsche: The Revolution in Nineteenth-Century
Thought*. New York: Columbia University Press, 1964.

Lukács, Georg. *History and Class Consciousness: Studies in Marxist Dialectics*.
1923. Translated by Rodney Livingstone. Cambridge, MA: MIT Press, 1971.

Lurie, Alison. *The Subversive Power of Children's Literature*. Boston: Little,
Brown, 1990.

Lyman, Rick. 'Movie Stars Fear Inroads by Upstart Digital Actors.' *New York
Times*, 8 July 2001.

Lyotard, Jean-François. *Discours, figure*. Paris: Klincksieck, 1971.

Macready, William Charles. *The Journal of William Charles Macready,
1832–1851*. Edited by J.C. Trewin. Carbondale: Southern Illinois University
Press, 1967.

Maeterlinck, Maurice. *Les aveugles*. 4th edition. Brussels: Paul Lacomblez, 1892.

– 'Le tragique quotidian.' In *Le trésor des humbles*. Paris: Société du Mercure
de France, 1894.

Marx, Karl. *Capital*. Vol. 1. Translated by Ben Fowkes. London: Penguin, 1976.

Matthews, Brander. *The Principles of Playmaking and Other Discussions of the
Drama*. New York: Scribner, 1919.

Mauss, Marcel. *The Gift: Forms and Functions of Exchange in Archaic Societies*.
Translated by Ian Cunnison. New York: W.W. Norton & Co., 1967.

Meisel, Martin. *Realizations: Narrative, Pictorial, and Theatrical Arts in
Nineteenth-Century England*. Princeton: Princeton University Press, 1983.

Melville, Herman. 'Hawthorne and His Mosses.' *The Literary World* (New
York), 17 and 24 August 1850.

Merleau-Ponty, Maurice. 'Eye and Mind.' In *The Primacy of Perception*, edited
by James M. Edie, translated by Carleton Dallery. Evanston: Northwestern
University Press, 1964.

– *Phenomenology of Perception*. Translated by Colin Smith. New York:
Routledge, 1989.

Mitchell, W.J.T. *Picture Theory: Essays on Verbal and Visual Representation*.
Chicago: University of Chicago Press, 1994.

Montaigne, Michel de. 'On Cannibals.' In *Essays*, translated by J.M. Cohen,
105–19. London: Penguin Books, 1958.

Montrose, Louis Adrian. '"Shaping Fantasies": Figurations of Gender and
Power in Elizabethan Culture.' In *Representing the English Renaissance*,
edited by Stephen Greenblatt, 31–64. Berkeley: University of California
Press, 1988.

Moran, Dermot. *Introduction to Phenomenology*. London: Routledge, 2000.

Nussbaum, Martha. *Love's Knowledge: Essays on Philosophy and Literature*. New York: Oxford University Press, 1990.

Oppenheim, Lois. *The Painted Word: Samuel Beckett's Dialogue with Art*. Ann Arbor: University of Michigan Press, 2000.

Paik, Karen, and Leslie Iwerks. *To Infinity and Beyond! The Story of Pixar Animation Studios*. New York: Chronicle, 2007.

Pater, Walter. *The Renaissance: Studies in Art and Poetry, the 1893 Text*. Berkeley: University of California Press, 1980.

Perez, Gilberto. *The Material Ghost: Films and Their Medium*. Baltimore: Johns Hopkins University Press, 1998.

Pirandello, Luigi. *Six Characters in Search of an Author and Other Plays*. Translated by Mark Musa. London: Penguin Books, 1995.

Pixar. http://www.pixar.com/companyinfo/history/1984.html (accessed 15 June 2005).

Plato. *The Symposium*. In *The Dialogues of Plato*, translated by Benjamin Jowett, 4 volumes, 1: 479–555. Oxford: Oxford University Press, 1953.

– *The Symposium of Plato*. Translated by B. Jowett. Boston: Branden, 1983.

Price, David A. *The Pixar Touch: The Making of a Company*. New York: Vintage, 2009.

Quigley, Austin. *The Modern Stage and Other Worlds*. New York: Methuen, 1985.

Rabaté, Jean-Michel. *The Ghosts of Modernity*. Gainesville: University Press of Florida, 1996.

Racine, Jean. *Athalie*. In *Théatre complet de Jean Racine*, 4: 290–440. Paris: Librairie Ch. Delgrave, 1882.

Riquelme, John Paul. *Harmony of Dissonances: T.S. Eliot, Romanticism, and Imagination*. Baltimore: Johns Hopkins University Press, 1991.

– 'Shalom/Solomon/*Salomé*: Modernism and Wilde's Aesthetic Politics.' *Centennial Review* 39, no. 3 (Fall 1995): 575–610.

Roach, Joseph. *The Player's Passion: Studies in the Theory of Acting*. Newark: University of Delaware Press, 1985.

Robinson, David. *Chaplin: His Life & Art*. New York: Da Capo Press, 1994.

Rosenberg, Alan, and Gerald E. Myers, eds. *Echoes from the Holocaust: Philosophical Reflections on a Dark Time*. Philadelphia: Temple University Press, 1989.

Ruskin, John. *The Art Criticism of John Ruskin*. Edited by Robert L. Herbert. New York: Da Capo Press, 1964.

Sarcey, Francisque. *Essai d'une esthétique de théâtre*. 1876. In *Quarante ans de théâtre*, 8 volumes, 1: 119–58. Paris: Bilbliothèque des Annales, 1900.

Sartre, Jean-Paul. *L'Imaginaire, psychologie phénoménologique de l'imagination*. Paris: Gallimard, 1940.

Scarry, Elaine. *The Body in Pain: The Making and Unmaking of the World.* New York: Oxford University Press, 1985.

– *Dreaming by the Book.* Princeton: Princeton University Press, 2001.

– *Resisting Representation.* New York: Oxford University Press, 1994.

Schaeffer, Jean-Marie. *Art of the Modern Age: Philosophy of Art from Kant to Heidegger.* Translated by Steven Rendall. Princeton: Princeton University Press, 2000.

Schechner, Richard. *Environmental Theater.* 1973. Reprinted, New York: Applause Books, 1994.

Schopenhauer, Arthur. *The World as Will and Representation.* Translated by E.F.J. Payne. New York: Dover, 1958.

Scofield, Martin. *The Ghosts of* Hamlet: *The Play and Modern Writers.* Cambridge: Cambridge University Press, 1980.

Shakespeare, William. *The Riverside Shakespeare.* Boston: Houghton Mifflin, 1974.

Shattuck, Charles. *The Hamlet of Edwin Booth.* Chicago: University of Illinois Press, 1969.

Sibony, Daniel. 'Hamlet: A Writing-Effect.' In *Literature and Psychoanalysis: The Question of Reading: Otherwise,* edited by Shoshana Felman, 53–85. Baltimore: Johns Hopkins University Press, 1982.

Smith, Adam. *The Theory of Moral Sentiments.* Amherst, NY: Prometheus, 2000.

Smith, Matthew Wilson. *The Total Work of Art: From Bayreuth to Cyberspace.* New York: Routledge, 2007.

Sofer, Andrew. *The Stage Life of Props.* Ann Arbor: University of Michigan Press, 2003.

Sorensen, Roy. *Seeing Dark Things: A Philosophy of Shadows.* New York: Oxford University Press, 2008.

Souriau, Étienne. 'Time in the Plastic Arts.' *Journal of Aesthetics and Art Criticism* 7 (1949): 294–307.

Stanislavski, Konstantin. *An Actor Prepares.* Translated by Elizabeth Reynolds Hapgood. New York: Theatre Arts Books, 1936.

– *Building a Character.* Translated by Elizabeth Reynolds Hapgood. New York: Theatre Arts Books, 1949.

– *My Life in Art.* Translated by J.J. Robbins. 1924. Reprinted, New York: World Publishing Co., 1956.

States, Bert O. *Great Reckonings in Little Rooms: On the Phenomenology of Theater.* Berkeley: University of California Press, 1985.

Stevens, Wallace. 'An Ordinary Evening in New Haven.' In *The Palm at the End of the Mind,* edited by Holly Stevens, 331. New York: Random House, 1972.

Strindberg, August. *The Ghost Sonata.* In *Plays: One,* translated by Michael Meyer, 155–91. London: Methuen, 1964.

– 'A Glance into Space.' In *Selected Essays by August Strindberg,* translated by Michael Robinson. Cambridge: Cambridge University Press, 1996.

– *Inferno and From an Occult Diary.* Translated by Mary Sandbach. London: Penguin Books, 1979.

Sutzkever, Abraham. 'A Wagon of Shoes.' In *Selected Poetry and Prose,* translated by Barbara and Benjamin Harshav, 151–3. Berkeley: University of California Press, 1991.

Szondi, Peter. *Theory of the Modern Drama.* Edited and translated by Michael Hays. Minneapolis: University of Minnesota Press, 1987.

Taylor, Charles. *Hegel and Modern Society.* Cambridge: Cambridge University Press, 1979.

– *Sources of the Self: The Making of the Modern Identity.* Cambridge, MA: Harvard University Press, 1989.

Trilling, Lionel. *Sincerity and Authenticity.* Cambridge, MA: Harvard University Press, 1971.

Turits, Michael. 'Moment of Impact: Three Air-Crashes.' *1-800* (Fall 1989): 33–8.

Turner, Victor. *Drama, Fields, and Metaphors: Symbolic Action in Human Society.* Ithaca: Cornell University Press, 1974.

Valency, Maurice. *The End of the World: An Introduction to Contemporary Drama.* New York: Oxford University Press, 1980.

Weiner, Annette B. *Inalienable Possessions: The Paradox of Keeping-While-Giving.* Berkeley: University of California Press, 1992.

White, Hayden. *Figural Realism.* Baltimore: Johns Hopkins University Press, 1999.

Wilde, Oscar. *The Complete Works of Oscar Wilde.* New York: Harper & Row, 1989.

Wilson, Edmund. *Axel's Castle: A Study in the Imaginative Literature of 1870–1930.* New York: Modern Library, 1996.

Wilson, J. Dover. 'Introduction.' In *Lewes Lavater: Of Ghosts and Spirites Walking by Nyght* 1572, edited by J. Dover Wilson and May Yardley, vii–xxviii. Oxford: Oxford University Press, 1929.

– *What Happens in* Hamlet. Cambridge: Cambridge University Press, 1937.

Wordsworth, William. *The Poetical Works of William Wordsworth.* 5 volumes. Oxford: Clarendon Press, 1949.

Worthen, W.B. *Modern Drama and the Rhetoric of Theater.* Berkeley: University of California Press, 1992.

Young, James E. *The Texture of Memory.* New Haven: Yale University Press, 1993.

Zemeckis, Robert. 'Behind the Scenes.' http://disney.go.com/disneypictures/achristmascarol/#/christmas_present/ (accessed 15 January 2010).

# Index

economic exchange. *See* capitalism; commodities

ekphrastic logic, 14, 15

electric light, 41

electron, 63, 64

Eliot, T.S., 40–1, 63; 'The Love Song of J. Alfred Prufrock,' 41; *Murder in the Cathedral*, 40; *The Waste Land*, 118

Elizabeth I, queen of England, 31

Ellmann, Richard, 62

Elohist, 8

Emerson, Ralph Waldo, 63

emotions: as inarticulate, 69–70; *Toy Story* toys and, 98

empathy, seeing with, 22, 70

empiricism, 14–15

*Endgame* (Beckett), 76–7, 85–6, 92, 95, 96, 133n32; flatness figuration and, 80–2

ends, origins and, 99, 102

Enlightenment, 9, 59, 63

epistemology, 11, 43, 64, 68, 85, 92

essence: of art, 72, 76, 77; indeterminacy of, 80; of love, 35

ethical values, measurement of, 27

evil, 30

exchange, 21–2, 107; commensurability in, 24–31. *See also* capitalism; gift-giving

existence, indeterminacy of, 80

expressionism, 44

expressive theory, 39, 62, 66, 76

eye. *See* vision

eye of the mind. *See* mind's eye

Fackenheim, Emil, 74

fathers: Oedipus and, 107, 108; Shakespeare and, 24–5, 26, 31, 32–3, 34, 105 (*see also* Ghost of Hamlet's father)

Felstiner, John, 133n35

Ficino, Marcilio: *Commentary on Plato's Symposium on Love*, 22, 23, 36

figurative language, 45

*Film* (Beckett), 65, 78, 82–4, 86, 88, 93, 94; Chaplin iconography and, 83–4; questions of flatness and, 66, 67, 82–3, 92

films, 12, 18; camera use and, 117–18, 139n21; digital 3D and, 3–6, 10, 12, 117–18; physical reality and, 83; representation and, 66–7, 68. *See also* computer animation

*Final Fantasy: The Spirits Within* (film), 139n11

flatness, 90, 92, 94, 95–8; death associated with, 86–7, 88, 94; eyes and, 73, 96; film images and, 67, 68; physical-metaphysical, 18, 66, 76; pictorial art and, 18, 66, 71, 72, 77–8, 81–3, 87, 96, 130n2; spectres and, 66; temporality and, 81–2; *Toy Story* films and, 97–8

Ford, John, 113

form: of forms, 105; Romantic theory of, 85

form-content dialectic, 63, 73, 78–80, 132n32

Foucault, Michel, 9, 13

foundational narratives, 7–8

frame: flatness and, 77; shift in use of term, 77; theatrical stage and, 68, 71–2, 76

Frank, Joseph: *The Widening Gyre*, 124n1

Frankfurt School, 9

French Revolution, theatrical impact of, 43, 44

Freud, Sigmund, 9, 111; 'The Uncanny,' 121–2n18; unconscious in *Hamlet* and, 40

Greenblatt, Stephen, 27, 28; *Hamlet in Purgatory,* 93–4, 140n22
grief, commensurability of, 24, 25

Hall, Susanna (Shakespeare's daughter), 31
Hallward, Basil, 57
*Hamlet* (Shakespeare), 37–64; Bernhardt's portrayal of Hamlet and, 61; Booth's production of, 41, 42, 48; closet scene of, 8, 47–9, 53; generosity and, 35–6; Globe theatre performances of, 44; interpreters of inner life and, 38–41, 65, 92, 125n12; introspection and, 69, 84; invisible made visible and, 39, 45; Joyce on central problem of, 56, 105; measurement of love and, 24; mirror metaphor and, 39; modern image of, 55–6, 125n1; observers and observed and, 6; play-within-play and, 35–6, 60, 61, 64; problems of knowing and, 44–5; psychoanalytic readings of, 40, 125n11; Romantic interpretations of, 12, 17, 18, 37–49, 51, 55, 65, 125n12; theological confusion about, 8; 'thing of nothing' and, 23; ways of seeing and, 42–3, 51. *See also* Ghost of Hamlet's Father
happiness, 22
Hawthorne, Nathaniel, 125n1
Hayter, Stanley William, 132n31
Heaney, Seamus: *Station Island,* 93
hearing, 86, 136n69
Hegel, G.W.F., 59, 60, 62, 63, 64, 69, 72, 73, 85; *The Phenomenology of Mind,* 37, 38–9
Heidegger, Martin, 72, 79, 135n48; Being-being(s) distinction and,

75; being-in-the-world and, 76; object-thing distinction and, 11, 71, 75; 'Origin of the Work of Art,' 75–6
Heisenberg, Werner: uncertainty principle, 64, 73
Heller, Erich, 125n12
Herod, 58, 59–60, 61
Hillman, David, 39
history, representation of, 74
Holocaust, 67, 74, 134–5n47
Homer: *Odyssey,* 7–8; Proteus legends and, 105; visual description and, 7–8, 14
homogeneity: distinction vs, 24, 25, 27, 29; of love, 34
Horkheimer, Max, 9
*Howdy, Sheriff Woody!* (book), 104
human interiority: authentic self and, 36; Beckett's approach to, 18–19, 66, 68, 80–6, 92; camera obscura as metaphor for, 126–7n29; creative role of, 63–4; ghostliness of, 69–70; *Hamlet* as representation of, 38–49, 65, 92, 125n12; Merleau-Ponty theory of, 75; new nineteenth-century views on, 41, 63; Pixar-Disney movies and, 99, 106; radical positivism vs, 91; relationship with other and, 40, 45 (*see also* subject-object correspondence); representation problems of, 8, 18, 19, 40, 48, 54–5, 69, 92; science-based visualization of, 52; of seeing, 3–4, 38, 44, 45–6, 50, 51, 63–4, 127n34; theatrical representation of, 18, 21, 37, 40, 41, 45, 48, 54–5, 65, 66, 68–71, 81–2, 84; truth and, 68, 69, 70; visual arts and, 66–7, 84, 86, 88. *See also* imagination; self